P9-AQH-541

WITHDRAWN

PRAISE FOR

EVERYTHING I LEARNED ABOUT RACISM I LEARNED IN SCHOOL

"Through honest and powerful vignettes, Jewell's latest stitches together a collective memoir of formative experiences of educational racism and American schooling. These bold tales of truth-telling are interspersed with historical facts that emphasize and contextualize the reality that, while experiences of racism in educational systems evolve with each generation, one constant is that schools are microcosms of larger systems of inequality and institutional oppression in the world beyond classroom walls. Unapologetic and unflinching: a critical read."

—*Kirkus Reviews* (starred review)

"Frequently in conversations around diversity in children's books, we hear use of the Dr. Rudine Sims Bishop metaphor that invokes 'mirrors, windows, and sliding glass doors.' This nonfiction compilation of narratives from writers of myriad ethnic and racial backgrounds—all around their experiences with racism as they attended American schools—will serve as a reflective validator for some, a view into a different experience for others, and an entry point for both connection and correction for readers overall. It's a text that should be added to high school curriculum lists across the nation."

—Nic Stone, #1 *New York Times* bestselling author of
How to Be a (Young) Antiracist

"The powerful tradition of Baldwin's loving call to critique echoes in this brilliant chorus of voices Tiffany Jewell gathers to speak about the experiences of children of the Global Majority in schools in America. *Everything I*

Learned About Racism I Learned in School is that rare gift that inspires, challenges, and dares us to 'envision what freedom in schools could be.' I want to share this book with every student and educator in America."

—Brendan Kiely, *New York Times* bestselling author of
The Other Talk: Reckoning with Our White Privilege

"Tiffany Jewell has a gift for getting to the guts of the thing with startling brevity and clarity—*Everything I Learned About Racism I Learned in School* is no exception. This is an essential book which examines not just the 'why' of racism but the deeply important 'how.'"

—Olivia A. Cole, author of *The Truth About White Lies*

"What an incredibly powerful book. This is a searing, gut-punching gift of a collection that will dwell in readers' souls—it took my breath away. Each of these short pieces is a poignant and powerful affirmation of our shared humanity; they offer multiple opportunities for honest and meaningful teaching and learning in and out of the classroom, for conversation among peers, between generations, and across boundaries. Essential. In the heart-break of accounts of trauma, microaggressions, and major cruelty, I found hope that those who might recognize themselves and their lives on these pages will be empowered, will find community and affirmation. But while there is pain on the pages, the overwhelming message, the ultimate story of this dynamic and beautiful anthology, is one of justice. *Everything I Learned About Racism I Learned in School* is an essential text for life, offering a diverse array of opportunities for us to not just see a more just world, but to take action in our own lives to create one."

—Olugbemisola Rhuday-Perkovich, coauthor of
The Sun Does Shine: An Innocent Man, a Wrongful Conviction, and the Long Path to Justice

"Tiffany Jewell continues to be a leader in anti-bias antiracist education. Although written for young people, *Everything I Learned About Racism I Learned in School* is a master class for teachers and parents on how to recognize inequities in the classroom and, more importantly, how to begin confronting and course correcting generations of systemic racism in education. Reading about the harmful and heartbreaking experiences that some of this country's most beloved authors, educators, and activists endured moved me to tears. Because their stories were reminders of the injustice that I also faced as a student, and how it shaped the trajectory of my personal and professional pursuits. *Everything I Learned About Racism I Learned in School* is a reminder of why it's our individual and collective responsibility to empower young people to think critically about their education and challenge the inequities that have plagued the American educational system for far too long."

—Christine Platt, author and literacy advocate

PRAISE FOR *THIS BOOK IS ANTI-RACIST*

#1 *New York Times* Bestseller
#1 Indie Bestseller

"Equips young people with the tools they need."
—*Time*

"Helps young people learn in a gentle, thoughtful way."
—*USA Today*

"I know firsthand the profound impact
Tiffany Jewell's teachings have. Now young people everywhere can benefit."
—Jarrett J. Krosoczka, National Book Award finalist
and author of *Hey, Kiddo*

"Clear, compelling language. Thoughtful, energizing."
—*Publishers Weekly* (starred review)

"Has something for all young people no matter what stage
they are at in terms of awareness."
—*Kirkus Reviews* (starred review)

"Successfully combines personal experience and
social and historical issues."
—*School Library Journal* (starred review)

HB 12 12 2023 0412

EVERYTHING I LEARNED ABOUT RACISM I LEARNED IN SCHOOL

EVERYTHING I LEARNED ABOUT RACISM I LEARNED IN SCHOOL

Tiffany Jewell

VERSIFY

An Imprint of HarperCollinsPublishers

Versify® is an imprint of HarperCollins Publishers.

Everything I Learned About Racism I Learned in School
Copyright © 2024 by Tiffany Jewell
"Amelia's Story" copyright © 2024 by Amelia A. Sherwood. "Other" copyright © 2024 by Randy Ribay. "Rebekah's Story" copyright © 2024 by Rebekah Borucki. "The Discipline Problem" and "Together, Everyone Achieves More" copyright © 2024 by Roberto Germán. "Self(less) Portrait: A Kind of One-Act Play" copyright © 2024 by Minh Lê. "Emmanuel's Story" copyright © 2024 by Emmanuel. "What I've Learned About Racism" copyright © 2024 by James Bird. "What I Remember (Part One)" and "What I Remember (Part Two)" copyright © 2024 by Lorena Germán. "Liz's Story" copyright © 2024 by Liz Sohyeon Kleinrock. "Stains We Can't Ignore" copyright © 2024 by Gary Gray Jr. "August's Story" copyright © 2024 by August. "The Othering" copyright © 2024 by Patrick Harris II. "The Fat Black Kid Who Flew" copyright © 2024 by shea wesley martin. "David's Letter" copyright © 2024 by David Ryan Barcega Castro-Harris. "Torrey's Story" copyright © 2024 by Torrey Maldonado. "Ozy's Story" and "Ozy's Letter" copyright © 2024 by Ozy Aloziem. "Notes on Schooling" copyright © 2024 by Gayatri Sethi. "The Story of Doña Ana, Doña Dulce María, and Dulce-Marie" copyright © 2024 by Dulce-Marie Flecha. "School Is the World" copyright © 2024 by Joanna Ho.
Illustrations © 2024 by George McCalman
The names of some of the individuals featured throughout this book have been changed.
All rights reserved. Printed in the United States of America. No part of this book may be used or reproduced in any manner whatsoever without written permission except in the case of brief quotations embodied in critical articles and reviews. For information address HarperCollins Children's Books, a division of HarperCollins Publishers, 195 Broadway, New York, NY 10007.
www.epicreads.com

Library of Congress Control Number: 2023936927
ISBN 978-0-35-863831-5

Typography and art by George McCalman
23 24 25 26 27 LBC 5 4 3 2 1

First Edition

To all the students in all the schools across the country:
You are bold, you are brave, you are whole, and you deserve
institutions that honor you as you are

CONTENTS

My High School

My College

INTRO
DUC

INTRODUCTION

I have always loved learning. I think that's why I liked school so much.

I liked having a place to go each day where I could be with friends. I liked the structure and routine. (I was a morning person!) I liked (and still do like) being challenged and having time and space to problem-solve.

I learned how to read in school. I remember our yellow phonics workbooks so clearly. I learned about the water cycle and recycling. I learned about the Hellenistic period and Gutenberg's printing press. I learned that a logarithm is an exponent. I learned a lot of things—and there was a lot that was missing.

For a while, I passively accepted things I learned in school as truth. I believed the stories we were taught. And what we read in the textbooks confirmed all we were told. I didn't seek information beyond the textbooks. For a while, I passively accepted all the things I learned in school. And then I started noticing.

I noticed a lot of things.

This book is about some of the things I noticed and how those things made school uncomfortable, unsafe, unfair, and unjust. It's part memoir, part anthology, part history, part social commentary, and part something else.

This book is mostly my school story.

I am a light-skinned Black biracial cisgender female who grew up in a midsize city in New York State. I do not have any disabilities, and English is my home language. I grew up in a racially expansive neighborhood of working-class poor folks. I lived with my mom and my twin sister in homes where there was heat and food. I attended our neighborhood public schools from preschool through high school. I'm a first-generation college graduate. I went to one private liberal arts college and then transferred to another.

This book is my journey through the public-school system. It includes some of my memories and some research, some facts, and some information. This book is me trying to make sense of the time I spent in school, from my first days of preschool through my college graduation.

This book is my coming to terms with the fact that just about everything I learned about racism, I learned in school.

This book is some of your school story too. It holds parts of our collective story of schooling in America.

So many of us have had similar experiences even though we were born in different decades, in different cities and towns, and to different families. Our school systems, whether public or private, traditional or alternative, are places where some of us experience racism and injustice and are witness to it daily.

This book also holds some stories from some of my friends, people I admire, and folks who write and share honestly. I asked them to write parts of their stories here because my words need not be the only ones. They can't be. I am not the only person who can tell this story.

I'm hoping you will write the next chapters, because this story isn't over. I hope you will be able to share your stories just like I am sharing some of mine.

This book is a reflection.

It is an exploration.

It's my truth and some of our shared truth.

It's a collection of small histories and stories.

This book is an unpacking and a processing and a trying to make sense of the world.

AMELIA

Amelia's Story

By Amelia A. Sherwood

Everything I learned about racism
I learned on top of my desk
White chalk scraping the board
In a Catholic school
While kneeling and praying to a white God

The brain is trained to protect you from the trauma
But your nervous system never forgets
Your body will always remember a reaction

I don't know the exact moment that schooling
Taught me to hate myself
But my body never forgot how to hide into the walls
How to cower
How to stay undetected and abandon the natural feeling of
    curiosity

I learned through the silence
That I couldn't be smart like Courtney
Pretty like Miriam
Or strong like Ryan
Wouldn't have perfect straight hair that could tuck around my ear
And no one to tell me that I was beautiful just the way I am
Not a single teacher told me I was intelligent

It was not what was said
It was what wasn't said

Everything I learned about racism
I learned in school
Forced to recite the preamble
Required to put my hand on my chest
Look up at the flag and let the Pledge
Of Allegiance fall out my mouth

I remember dressing up as Pilgrims and Native People
My savvy teacher putting the juice outside the windowsill so it
    could be cold
For the Thanksgiving celebration
I was in the first grade
I remember our white Spanish teacher told us to stop yelling out
    the window:

"Just because we are in the hood, doesn't mean you have to act
     like it."
I was in middle school

I remember the worst history teacher alive
Who kicked students out of his classroom
And I know he hated us
I was in high school

Everything I learned about anti-racism
and everything good about my people

I learned in my mama's house
I learned in a rural town outside of Philly
My mother always told me I was beautiful
Without saying a word
Professors taught me about the history of Africa before 1865
It was an actual course
A white Jewish woman, Professor Jontry, taught me how to
     organize
Dr. Babatunde set his expectations high for me
Dr. Poe gave me a middle-school African American history
     book
"I know you didn't learn anything about yourself, so let's start
     from the beginning."
Dr. Milluete fired me up and taught me to put my poster over
     my face at a protest

Everything I learned about anti-racism
And everything good about my people
Was a coming back home
A renewal

It is a deep practice now
To jolt myself out of what I have internalized
It is a practice or reimagining a world where history is not
    tainted
Where learners are able to be critical and curious
To feel affirmed
To be free

WHAT I LEARNED ABOUT MY LABEL

Once upon a time, my school district labeled my race as *White*.

My mom is White. Blond hair and blue eyes, she came to the United States from England on a big ship when she was a little kid.

My dad is Black. Brown hair and brown eyes (just like mine), he grew up in different cities and towns along the East Coast.

I am not White. Neither is my twin sister.

The label I prefer for my racialized identity is *Black biracial*.

When I entered the school system, I called myself *mixed*. And when my mom had to fill out our registration paperwork, she chose two boxes whenever she could, ticking both *Black* and *White* on our school forms. This went for any government forms too. If she had to make only one choice, she chose the box marked *other*. There weren't many options in the 1980s. Really, there still aren't today. In fact, it wasn't until the year 2000 that folks could finally identify with more than one race in the government census.

Someone somewhere in our school's administration, maybe even someone at the district level, decided to label my twin and me as White kids.

Our district needed more White kids to balance things out in our school that was considered "racially imbalanced." I don't know for sure, but I do wonder if my twin and I, both with lighter skin and living with our White mom, helped balance the school's quotas.

My sister and I were labeled White. Maybe whoever put that label in our files thought they were helping our school or the district out. Maybe they did it because someone with even more power told them to. Or, even worse, maybe it was done without any thought, with no one recognizing the importance of families having the autonomy and the ability to label themselves.

***

We didn't find out about our racialized labels until we were in high school. For fourteen years, my twin and I (and probably a bunch of other biracial and light-skinned kids in our city district before and after us) walked through our "racially imbalanced" schools with the privileges of a label that didn't fit and that not everyone got.

My high school embarked on a block-scheduling experiment. We were the first in our district to do so. Classes went from being forty minutes every day to eighty minutes on a

9

rotating four-day cycle. I liked the new schedule.

To help keep us organized, our school gave each student a planner. It was small, about the size of a paperback book, bound with a white plastic spiral. It had a plastic maroon and white cover with our school mascot on it. The little agenda books (that's what we called them) included calendars for each month, a weekly spread with space to write our assignments in each day, and monthly bathroom passes. We got only twenty passes each month. (Even though there are sometimes more than twenty school days in the month and being able to go to the restroom multiple times during a day is a right you should never be denied.) We were not to lose our agenda books. They were our school lives in cheap little laminated spiral-bound books.

Each had a little sticker label on the top right corner with the student's name and homeroom number. It also had a little letter, either *W, O, P,* or *N.* The *W* was for *White,* the *O* for *other,* the *P* for *Puerto Rican,* and the *N* for *Negro.* We didn't know about our racial labels. We didn't know that we were each put into one of only four categories. We didn't know that our school district was okay with using the *very* outdated (by over twenty-five years) term *Negro* rather than *African American* or *Black.* We didn't know that we could be only Puerto Rican, White, Negro, or other, even though we were so much more than that. When we found out, we were outraged.

The district administration said the letters, which they called "racial identification," should never have been included on our agenda books and that it was a computer mistake. *But where else were these letters being used?* It wasn't the computers that labeled each one of us. People did that. *What other decisions were made about our identities?* When asked about the labels, the superintendent didn't have much to say other than that the racial–identification letters didn't serve any purpose on our agenda books. *But where did they serve a purpose? And what was that purpose?* At the time, the district was using a twenty-five-year-old coding system and blamed that for its use of the outdated and limited categories. Collectively, we students were upset. We were mad. I was confused. The letter next to my name was *W.* And that wasn't me. I knew who I was, but the district told me otherwise.

WHAT I LEARNED ABOUT WHITENESS

Our labels follow us around. Whether we want them to be there or not, they are.

My racial label silently followed me around from preschool to middle school to high school.

Those labels kept us divided and disconnected. Whether I approved of my label or not, it followed me from classroom to classroom and from school to school. Because of our *W, O, P,* and *N* labels, some of us were given privileges, power, access, and advantages and some of us were never even given a chance.

My district gave me Whiteness. And the schools I attended treated me like I was a White kid. I had privileges and immunity that a lot of my classmates and peers did not get:

I was enrolled in Advanced Placement classes, which were filled predominantly with White kids. On average, White students are six times more likely to take an AP course than biracial or multiracial students in my old school district. Nationally, Black and American Indian students make up the smallest percentage of students enrolled in AP courses. In the 2017–2018 school year, less than 4 percent of students enrolled in AP classes were Black. More than 52 percent of students enrolled in Advanced Placement courses are White; Black students make up only about 9 percent of the students enrolled.

I was never suspended. I was never sent to detention. Black students in my old school district are nearly two times more likely to be suspended than their White classmates. For out-of-school suspension in my city, Black students are suspended at a much higher rate than any other race or ethnic group. Nationally, the rate of out-of-school suspensions are much higher for Black students than for any other racial or ethnic group. In the 2017–2018 school year, Black students made up 15 percent of student enrollment in schools and 39 percent of the students who were expelled from school. That means they were more than twice as likely to be suspended than students

NATIONAL BLACK STUDENT ENROLLMENT

BLACK STUDENTS ENROLLED

BLACK STUDENTS EXPELLED

of any other race or ethnicity.

I was tracked into the "best" classes with the most resources. I was college-bound before I even knew I wanted to go to college. (And because of this, my twin and I were the first in our family to graduate from four-year colleges.) Latine and Black students are considered academically "behind" White students in my old school district (by 1.6 and 1.3 grades, respectively).

I graduated from high school as a member of the National Honor Society. The graduation rate in my old district is low. While about 83 percent of students graduate from high school in New York State, in my home city only about 72 percent of students graduated in the 2021–2022 school year. Nationally, students graduate from high school at a rate of about 86 percent. My home city's rate of graduation is much lower than the state and national averages.

I was encouraged to go to college. The high-school guidance counselor met with me and helped our family figure out how to apply for financial aid and scholarships. Not going to college was never an option. The New York State average of high-school students who go directly to college upon graduating is about 72 percent. In my home city, the percentage of students who went directly to college was 46 percent, much lower than the state and national average of about 63 percent.

I was believed. I was trusted (implicitly) by teachers and school administrators. I was encouraged to always do well and succeed.

RANDY

Other

By Randy Ribay

"What are you?"

This is a question that has followed me throughout my life, but especially when I was growing up in the 1990s in Rochester Hills, Michigan. It was (and is) an overwhelmingly white suburb of Detroit, the city where Madonna spent her childhood.

"What are you?"

My white friends and classmates and teammates asked. Teachers and coaches asked. Friends' parents asked. Strangers asked when my family was shopping at Meijer or my siblings and I were playing basketball or tennis at Borden Park. The MEAP and SAT and ACT asked—although the Scantrons never offered bubbles that I could fill in confidently with my no. 2 pencil.

"What are you?"

They meant my race, of course. I was not white or Black; they knew that much right away or they wouldn't have asked the question. Maybe I was some kind of Asian? I reminded them of Bruce Lee or Jackie Chan or Short Round or Data. Maybe Hispanic? Maybe some kind of mixture—that was it, right? Hard to say for sure with such ambiguous features, with sort of "almond" eyes, with skin whose brownness was seasonal.

"What are you?"

Often the question came immediately after people set eyes on me. Other times, they held it like a breath when they (tried to) read my last name. They couldn't place it, couldn't pronounce it correctly (even if they thought they could). Few and far between were the ones who asked how to say it, and even fewer and farther between were the ones who remembered how.

"What are you?"

They usually asked with idle curiosity, the casual insistence of those with the right to know anything they wanted. But sometimes there was an undercurrent (or overcurrent?) of frustration. Maybe they were upset that they could not define or categorize me, that my existence revealed the limits of their worldview, my presence the limits of their suburban paradise.

"What are you?"

People had a burning curiosity about my race, despite the fact we were (supposedly) living in the era of color blindness. My school, my parents, and the media aggressively taught us (mostly in February) that racism was over. The civil rights movement had (supposedly) accomplished its mission. Slavery and segregation and discrimination were (supposedly) relics of the past.

"What are you?"

They asked even though in the 1990s, it (supposedly) no longer mattered. Anyone could be anything they wanted. If someone never achieved their goals, it was because they were too lazy to work hard, too dumb to assimilate. If there were patterns of success or struggle across racial groups, it was because of differences in "culture."

"What are you?"

Look at Oprah. Look at all the (dead) rappers. Look at the NBA and the NFL and some of the MLB (but definitely not the NHL or NASCAR). Look at Tiger Woods. Look (not too closely, though) at *A Different World* and *The Fresh Prince of Bel-Air* and all those kung fu guys. Look at that one CEO. That one family living in a new McMansion built on the rich side of town. That one professor at Oakland University. That one doctor at Beaumont Medical Center. Look at the Burger King Kids Club and the Power Rangers and the Planeteers—one kid of each minority (but still several white kids)!

"What are you?"

Some who asked were living on land their ancestors had taken from the Potawatomi. A suburb whose population boomed because of white flight and redlining following the 1967 uprisings in Detroit. A city whose (few) Asian immigrants could likely trace their arrival to the Immigration and Nationality Act of 1965. A city to which my own family had moved after having lived in the mostly Black neighboring community of Pontiac during our first few years in this country. (The suburbs were "safer," the schools "better," the people "nicer," the community "cleaner." Everyone agreed. It was so obvious, it didn't even need to be said—still, though, they said it. A lot.)

What are you?

People did not want the answer. They could not comprehend its complexity. They'd already filed me under "other," and the details would evaporate into the air as soon as I spoke them.

What are you?

What was I?

Sick of that question. Sick of being asked about my race by white people who pretended they did not see race when it was all they saw if it was not white.

REBEKAH

Rebekah's Story

By Rebekah Borucki

Nuance was never a part of my public education experience. It happened, or it didn't. It was, or it wasn't. We were fed absolute facts, not up for debate. Both math and history got the same treatment. *George Washington Crossing the Delaware*, plus Operation Desert Storm, equaled "We live in the greatest country on earth." Everything we needed to know fit neatly into a set of boxes that we were expected to accept but never unpack or examine.

The student body was also expected to fit into boxes. You were smart, average, or "a special ed kid." You lived on one side of the tracks or the other. You were Black or White. Straight or, well, nobody was gay—some boxes weren't available to us. I suppose this system suited a lot of folks just fine, but it proved complicated (and confusing) to those of us born outside of what was definable, packageable. Checking multiple boxes was discouraged if it was an option at all.

I grew up in a village of brick row houses, where neighbors

19

felt more like extended family, and everyone knew each other's business. It felt safe and suffocating at the same time. The neighbors knew that my mother had a relationship with some shade of brown man and that I was the product of that indiscretion. They knew before I knew, and they talked about it even though I was never allowed.

"It smells like a nigger. Like you." She was five years old and lived on my block. We were born ten days apart in 1978, and we played together nearly every day—unsupervised, until the streetlights came on, you know, the good old days. I found a plastic ring on the ground and brought it to the sisters to show it off. I thought it was pretty; she said it smelled bad, like a nigger. I wouldn't know the depth of the meaning of that word for many years to come, and I certainly didn't know that I was one. I recalled a senile neighbor shouting it at my mother's best friend, Alpha, when she came to visit, but I couldn't quite place what it was that I had in common with her. It was apparent the triplets knew something that I didn't, but I didn't ponder it for too long. I tucked the information away, but it must have made an impression. Or is it trauma? That was the first time someone tagged me with a label I didn't understand, but it certainly wouldn't be the last. My light-brownness came up—and still comes up—a lot.

At five years old, my playmates and I were starting kindergarten and meeting kids from other neighborhoods for the first time. We were encouraged to play pretend; the girls were herded toward the kitchen set and the boys toward the trucks, and we organized our playgroups into "Mommy," "Daddy," "Sister," and "Baby." But my classmate, Tasha, and I couldn't be Mommy or Daddy or any part of the pretend family. Even though Tasha didn't smell funny to me, I found out that she was a nigger, just like me. And that meant that we, even though we were playing pretend, didn't have the qualities required to be part of the group. So again, like before with my mother's best friend, I found myself wondering what exactly made Tasha and me so much like each other but also so different from everyone else, and this time, unacceptable.

Boxes. That's when my education about boxes started, when I realized that nuance and overlap and complex definitions weren't a thing—for my classmates, or my teachers, or the world in which I found myself confined. Tasha and Alpha and me— we belonged in one box, and *they* lived in another, better box. As a mixed kid, I got put in a lot of boxes, but *they* got to pick them all. So, *they* put me in the White Box, the Black Box, and as I got older and found myself occupying predominately White spaces for work, the "I mean, you're not *BLACK* Black" box.

I wonder how that last one has been used so many times by so many people from vastly different backgrounds. I wonder where they learned it, which class it was that taught them what it meant to be White or Black or any other label and set of attributes they've accepted as truth. I'm still figuring it out, but I know my education started in kindergarten.

WHAT RACISM IS

The language we use is powerful.

The words we are taught from our earliest days hold incredible power. They shape the world around us and our understanding of it. The language we use can bring us together, and it can also exclude and divide us.

In this book, I talk about racism a lot. Having a clear definition of what racism is helps me understand this kind of injustice more clearly. Whenever I talk, think, and write about racism, I use the definition that was shared with me in an anti-racism training workshop years ago. Racism is *both* personal prejudice and bias *and* the systemic misuse and abuse of power by institutions.

Let's break it down, because this isn't the definition of racism we're often taught.

Everybody has prejudice and bias.

PREJUDICE is a belief, attitude, or feeling about a person or group of people that comes from not having the right information and believing the stereotypes you've heard, read about, and absorbed. Usually, you and other people are aware of your prejudices.

BIAS is a belief you have about a person, a group of people, a place, or a thing. Some biases are obvious, and you know what they are and that they exist. Other biases are hidden, and you are not always aware of what they are or why you have them.

We all make judgments. We all have opinions.

Sometimes, those opinions are based on our experiences and identities. Other times, those judgments, prejudices, and biases are based on stereotypes and misinformation that we absorb from the media and the world around us. They also come from the people we interact with, the places we frequent, the ways we are brought up by our caregivers, the information (and misinformation) we are exposed to, the things we're taught (and not taught) at school, and so many other sources. Sometimes our biases and prejudices are conscious, known to us, and we're very aware of them. Other times, they're not so obvious and we aren't always aware of why we believe the things we do. Regardless, racism is not just people holding prejudices and biases against others.

Sometimes, often, when we learn about racism, we learn only about the personal side. Prejudice is personal, and racism is much more than just personal interactions between people. It's a system that keeps people with Black and Brown skin (People of the Global Majority) oppressed. It's a system in which people with White and light skin have advantages over people with darker

23

GLOBAL MAJORITY

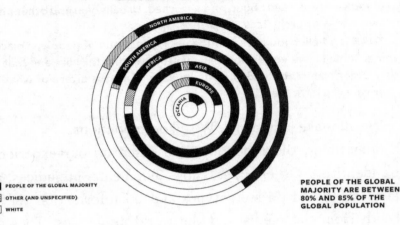

PEOPLE OF THE GLOBAL MAJORITY

OTHER (AND UNSPECIFIED)

WHITE

PEOPLE OF THE GLOBAL
MAJORITY ARE BETWEEN
80% AND 85% OF THE
GLOBAL POPULATION

skin. It's a system that keeps people divided from each other, and it has been doing so for hundreds and hundreds of years.

I first heard the term **PEOPLE OF THE GLOBAL MAJORITY** from a friend who worked closely with Dr. Barbara J. Love. I love this term and use it instead of **MINORITY**. The word **MINORITY** makes me feel small and unimportant. Using **PEOPLE OF THE GLOBAL MAJORITY** reminds me that I am a part of a whole big group of people around the world who are Black and Brown and make up the majority of the planet's population. It's empowering!

Racism is an unfair and unjust system.

Racism was created and is maintained to ensure that White people (as a whole group) have the most resources and power. Racism is a system that keeps BIPOC people and White people separated and divided. Within this system, Indigenous, Black, Latine, Asian, and other People of the Global Majority have less resources and power.

This was and is accomplished by creating unfair and unjust laws, rules, and policies and upholding them in traditions that have become part of our society.

Racism is (and was) accomplished through colonization.

COLONIZATION is accomplished when one group takes control of another by violence and force. Colonizers use brutality and manipulation to gain and maintain power and control over people, land, and resources. An example of this is when the U.S. government physically removed tens of thousands of Indigenous Native Americans from their homelands along the East Coast and forced them to go (mostly by foot) westward to reservations on undesirable land.

COLONIZATION

ACCOMPLISHED WHEN ONE GROUP TAKES CONTROL OF ANOTHER BY VIOLENCE AND FORCE

Racism is accomplished by the creation of a criminal justice system that unfairly and unjustly incarcerates Black people at a rate much higher than and disproportionate to White people. According to the Federal Bureau of Prisons, while Black folks represent about 12 percent of the adult population in the United States, they represent 38.4 percent of the federal prison population. And while Latine folks represent 19 percent of the adult population in the country, they represent about 30 percent of the federal prison population. Black people are arrested at a much higher and disproportionate rate than White people. For every 100,000 people, 6,109 Black folks are arrested while only 2,795 White folks are arrested. The adult population of White people in the United States is about 61 percent. Black folks are arrested more than twice as much as White folks. The disproportionality is unfair and unjust.

Racism is accomplished by local and federal governments demolishing predominantly Black, Brown, and Jewish neighborhoods and building highways to help White families who moved out of the cities access those cities with ease.

Racism is accomplished by banking institutions refusing to give loans to Black and Brown people, making it difficult for folks to buy homes and accrue wealth for generations.

Racism is accomplished by maintaining a health-care system that upholds the false belief that Black people have a higher tolerance for pain, which is why Black folks who give birth die during or after birth at a much higher rate than any other race. Black people are three times more likely to die from pregnancy-related causes than White folks. Native Americans and Native Alaskans are two times more likely to die from pregnancy-related causes. This is unfair and unjust.

Racism is accomplished through gentrification, pushing people out of their homes, communities, and neighborhoods.

GENTRIFICATION is when folks with wealth and resources buy homes, properties, and businesses in neighborhoods that are typically urban and poor. Neighborhoods are transformed, and because of the changes made (such as increases in rent, taxes, and mortgages), the original residents are often not able to stay in their neighborhoods. Gentrification can happen on small and large scales and has a lasting impact on community members.

GENTRIFICATION

WHEN FOLKS WITH WEALTH AND RESOURCES BUY HOMES, PROPERTIES, AND BUSINESSES IN NEIGHBORHOODS THAT ARE TYPICALLY URBAN AND POOR

Racism is accomplished by businesses refusing to interview or hire people because their names sound "too Black" or "too Asian" or "too ethnic." A recent study revealed that folks with names that sounded "too Black" had more than 2 percent less chance of being contacted by interviewers.

Racism is accomplished by businesses and institutions paying People of the Global Majority much less than they pay White men for doing the same (or more) work. For every dollar a White man made in 2020, Pacific Islander and Asian American women made on average eighty-five cents, Black women made sixty-four cents, multiracial Black women made sixty-three cents, Native American women made sixty cents, and Latine women made fifty-seven cents. This big difference in pay is unfair and unjust.

Racism is accomplished by politicians advocating for, supporting, and passing laws that remove books from our classrooms, schools, and libraries. These books are written by and about Black folks, trans folks, folks in the LGBTQIA+ community, Latine folks, Asian folks, folks of the Global Majority, and any other folks who don't fit neatly into the country's prevailing culture of dominance.

Racism is accomplished by books, magazines, television shows, and movies portraying White people as always kind, intelligent, and trustworthy and Black and Brown folks as unintelligent, violent, and unworthy of love.

Racism is accomplished by schools enforcing strict attendance policies without taking the whole lives of their students into account. A study by the California Department of Education in the 2017–2018 school year noted that, on average, 64

THE DIFFERENCE IN EXCUSED STUDENT ABSENCES

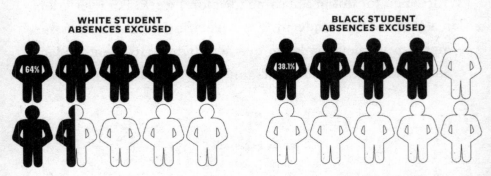

WHITE STUDENT ABSENCES EXCUSED — 64%

BLACK STUDENT ABSENCES EXCUSED — 38.1%

percent of absences for White students were excused, while only 38.1 percent of Black students' were. Student absences are excused for illness and other reasons that are approved by the school admin. Often, unexcused absences are caused by things beyond the students' control, like needing to help family out with childcare or having transportation issues. Unfortunately, as you may have experienced, students with unexcused absences might face disciplinary action, which can result in their being removed from the classroom or school.

Racism is accomplished by schools placing children in special-education classes because they are more comfortable speaking their home language than English.

Racism is accomplished by school districts and systems refusing to teach ethnic studies and teaching only a one-sided history that glorifies the accomplishments of mostly White men.

Racism is accomplished by schools *everywhere*, over and over again.

***

As soon as I started school, I was inundated with the ways that our country's education system colludes with and maintains the culture of White domination. It's unavoidable.

Without being explicitly taught, I learned:

. . . that I needed to get the best grades to be of worth and importance and that those grades would somehow still matter years after I'd finished with school (they actually don't);

. . . that practice makes perfect, and perfect was what I

should be, or at least strive to be;

. . . that I shouldn't make mistakes because if I did, I was the mistake and there was something wrong with me;

. . . that the people with the most power always knew what was best for me and for all of us and should be the ones to make all the decisions, even when those decisions kept us purposely divided;

. . . that success was about getting the highest grades and the most sports trophies, medals, and rewards rather than about how I treated other people and supported our community;

. . . that the most qualified and important books to read were the "classics" written by long-dead White male authors, like William Faulkner, William Shakespeare, and William Wordsworth;

. . . that my sentences and the way I spoke should always be grammatically correct according to the rules of the English language;

. . . that all stories worth telling should be written down in order to mean anything and matter;

. . . that I should never be emotional or I'd be dismissed as "too sensitive" or "angry" or "irrational," and that could lead to me being sent to the principal's office or detention;

. . . that the people who held the most power were the ones who were the most qualified to hold and *keep* that power;

. . . that I was supposed to trust the people with power implicitly.

Although it wasn't stated explicitly in the core curriculum or a textbook, I was taught that certain people—Indigenous people, Black people, Asian people, Latine people, People of the Global Majority—were the problem, because I learned to blame individual people (and groups of people) for racism and Islamophobia and antisemitism and transphobia and ableism and all injustice and oppression. But, really, people aren't the problem; it's the institutions that are.

MY HOME CITY

The stories you'll read in this book could have happened (and actually did happen) just about anywhere in the United States—in Massachusetts and Michigan, in California and Washington, DC, in Nebraska and Oregon. The parts of this schooling story that are mine take place in Syracuse, a midsize city in upstate New York with a population of just over 170,000. My home city sits in the middle of the Erie Canal route that once connected Albany and Buffalo. The summers are hot and humid, and the winters are cold and very snowy. A point of pride for my home city is its many Golden Snowball Awards and the title of "City with the Most Snow." (When I was in sixth grade, the city had 192 inches of snow in one winter!) We root for college athletes and treat them like they're professional players.

My home city has statistically been on the "decline" for many decades. Over 30 percent of its residents are living in poverty. The city is deeply divided and segregated; Interstate 81 strategically cuts through neighborhoods, following some families out to the neighboring suburbs and hemming other families in, close to the city's center.

MY

ELEME

ELEME

SC

NTARY

HOOL

MY CHILDHOOD NEIGHBORHOOD

My schooling journey started in 1984. (I know that was several decades ago, but trust me, schooling stories haven't changed that much!) Tina Turner's "What's Love Got to Do with It" was the number-one song in the country that year and my three-year-old self loved it.

The south side of the city was my home. The people who lived on the block felt like my extended family. My mom, twin, and I rented half of a two-family house. A couple of houses down from ours, on the right side, was an older couple from Ireland who had a cat named Kitty Kitty. Their grandchildren visited often, and though they were older, they joined in our play. A little farther down the road was where Josie's family lived. Their house was filled with cousins and older siblings who could go to the corner store on their own. In the opposite direction was another friend and his older brothers. Across the street was Cherisse and her mom; Joey and his family; and the man in the peach-colored house, who had several toy poodles that liked to bark at us.

I loved living on our block. We played on the sidewalk, in yards, and on each other's porches. Our caregivers never needed to set up playdates—we just left our homes and played. There was always someone to play with.

My elementary school was big—it had to be to accommodate between four and five hundred students. My twin and I went there from preschool all the way through sixth grade. Even though it was a magnet school (I'll tell you more about that in a bit!), it was our neighborhood school. It was only a few blocks away and it took us less than ten minutes to walk there. My mom never considered sending us to any other school. It was part of our neighborhood. It was where she and her siblings had gone. It was the only school we all knew.

The physical building was imposing with its sandy-colored brick walls. It stood two stories high with windows on most sides. There were multiple entrances to the school, and during my nine years there, I entered through each one of those doors. My classmates who took the bus to school were dropped off at the main entrance. A big, fenced-in green field with a slight slope greeted us as we approached the school every morning. There was a playground at the top of the field that included a blacktop and typical playground equipment—swings, a slide, and a climbing structure. Our school building took up a lot of space; it made up more than half the block.

The neighborhood the school sat in, on the south side, was predominantly Black and Brown families, working poor White folks, and old immigrant families. Our mom dropped us off at school, then walked up the street to catch the bus downtown to go to work. Our nana picked my twin and me up from school at the end of the day until the middle of second grade, when we started walking to her house on our own.

My kid world existed within those few blocks.

***

During the time I was in elementary school, about a third of the children in my city were living in poverty. (That's a lot!) My home city continues to have one of the highest rates of poverty in the country: over 40 percent of children there live in poverty. In 2016, the National Center for Education Statistics noted that about 19 percent of children (people under the age of eighteen) live in poverty in the United States. Black children and American Indian/Alaska Native children make up the highest number of children living in poverty (34 percent each of their respective populations). And 28 percent of Latine children live in poverty, 23 percent of Pacific Islander children live in poverty, and 19 percent of children who identify with two or more races live in poverty. White children and Asian/Asian American children make up 11 percent each of their respective populations. Currently, in the United States, more than thirty-seven million people are living in poverty.

The rate of poverty isn't a static or constant number. It can change from year to year due to different factors. In 2021, the rate of poverty among children was at a record low at 5.2 percent. In 2022, the rate more than doubled to 12.4 percent. This rise coincides with the expiration of state and federal government support that was offered to citizens during the COVID pandemic.

I want to pause for a moment and define what living in poverty means to me.

Living in poverty is not having enough because your people (your family, your ancestors, people who share similar social identities as you, and so on) and your community have been exploited and stripped of power and resources for years, decades, and centuries. It's when there has been little or, most likely, no redistribution of resources, wealth, and power, and no reparations have been made. Living in poverty often means having to rely on rations that are never quite enough from government agencies and nonprofits that feel the need to control the resources.

We existed in the WIC clinic. We pulled out food stamps at the grocery store. We had toys from the Christmas-toy giveaway. And we put our new school clothes on layaway.

Living in poverty does not mean you are dirty, violent, uneducated, and unloved!

In general, we are often encouraged to blame the people living in poverty rather than the misuse and abuse of power by the very institutions and systems that should keep us safe. Living in poverty is not having enough to meet your basic needs because your community and your people have been systematically and historically excluded, exploited, and stripped of resources and power for decades and centuries.

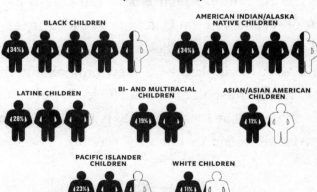

19% OF TOTAL CHILDREN
LIVING IN POVERTY IN THE U.S.
(UNDER 18 YEARS OLD)

BLACK CHILDREN (34%)

AMERICAN INDIAN/ALASKA NATIVE CHILDREN (34%)

LATINE CHILDREN (28%)

BI- AND MULTIRACIAL CHILDREN (19%)

ASIAN/ASIAN AMERICAN CHILDREN (11%)

PACIFIC ISLANDER CHILDREN (23%)

WHITE CHILDREN (11%)

WHAT I LEARNED ABOUT MAGNET SCHOOLS

I always thought I was a product of successful school–integration efforts. I started school thirty years after the *Brown v. Board of Education* Supreme Court ruling that declared segregation illegal.

I thought I was a part of a post–integration generation. (School segregation was illegal back in the 1980s and it still is today!) The neighborhood schools we attended felt racially expansive and diverse to me. A lot of my classmates were kids of the Global Majority, in particular Black kids. Most of our teachers were White, which is still the case today. About 79 percent of teachers in the United States identify as White. But we did have a couple of Black administrators, which felt radical in a way. In the United States, only about 10 percent of public–school principals are Black. (Over 77 percent are White.)

The truth is that I was actually part of the ongoing desegregation experiment in our city schools. The desegregation efforts of schools in our country were (and continue to be) slow, so slow.

I believed I was part of a post–integration generation because I had been taught that school integration happened in the past and far away from our city in central New York. The only school–integration stories I was familiar with were the ones that so many students in the United States get told.

I learned about *Brown v. Board of Education*.

I learned about Ruby Bridges and that in 1960, she was the first Black kid to integrate into a White school in Louisiana. She was only six and spent the first year being taught alone.

I learned about the Little Rock Nine, the first Black kids to integrate into a White school, Little Rock Central High School, in 1957.

The desegregation of schools was something I, a kid in the North, learned about as part of the past, something that had happened in the South and only in the South.

I never learned that segregation was a problem anywhere west or north of the Southern states. I never learned about what happened in the North—in particular, in the Northeast and in my own city—because there was this consistent and biased belief that things were always better in the North. But to this day, the majority of this country's most segregated school districts are in the Northeast and the Midwest. The most seg-regated school district in the country is in central New York, not too far away from where my own schooling journey began.

***

A little history:

In 1958, before I was born, even before my mom was born, my home city's school board approved the merging of two south-side schools. Some families and community members protested—no one wanted the center of their community to shift and move and change. But despite the protests, the merger happened.

The Brighton School, which was founded in 1842, was one of the oldest schools in the city. The school building was close to a main road. The traffic was loud, and the location was not safe for children. The plan was for students and families from the Brighton School to merge with the nearby McKinley School community. Named after the twenty-fifth president of our country, the McKinley School had been established in 1904. The schools were located just a few blocks from each other. In the early 1960s, the school merger was complete, and McKinley-Brighton Elementary School came to be.

When my mom and her sister moved to the city in the mid-1960s, they attended their neighborhood school. The newly merged school was where they went to learn and make new friends. It was also where they lost their British accents and became American kids.

Later, our neighborhood school became a magnet school. Its specialty, or "magnetic draw," was that it offered more math and science instruction than other elementary schools in the district.

In 1976, our school district asked teachers to volunteer to transfer to different schools in hopes of ending "racial isolation"

42

and segregation. Only 9 of 538 teachers volunteered to move to different schools. The majority of the schools in our district had no Black or Brown teachers of the Global Majority at all. That same year, the district implemented compulsory (mandatory) busing for some students living in the city's south side. Some students (mostly Black kids from schools that were predominantly Black) were assigned to schools that weren't in their neighborhoods, so they had to be bused there. Busing was another solution to fix our segregated schools, and like the teacher transfers, it wasn't very popular. So our city school district looked to another solution to solve the problem of our segregated schools—magnet schools.

In the late 1960s and early 1970s, magnet schools started to pop up around the country. Magnet schooling helped diversify neighborhood schools so they weren't filled with only White students or only Black students or only Latine students or only Asian students or only Indigenous students or only Brown students. (But the focus then was, too often, only on the racial binary of Black folks and White folks.) Because voluntary busing from one neighborhood school to another wasn't a popular choice for most White families, school districts tried to find ways to entice them to send their kids to schools in neighborhoods that were not predominantly White.

The focus was almost always on keeping the White families happy so they would keep their kids in the public schools. The focus was almost always on the White families and never on what Black and Brown families wanted and needed.

Magnet schools are like magnets—ideally, they pull people toward them. They are schools of choice. Families apply for admission to a magnet school based on its specialty—whether that's STEAM (science, technology, engineering, art, and mathematics), fine arts, performing arts, International Baccalaureate, world languages, or something else. Unlike neighborhood schools that you can walk to or ride your bike to, magnet schools might be across town. Students who attend magnet schools come from all over the city and live in different neighborhoods. My district (like so many others) found a way to get White families in particular to opt in and choose to bus their children to schools (like my neighborhood school) throughout the city.

I was a part of the new magnet-schooling experiment.

My elementary school had "too many Black kids." When I was in second grade, the Black student population was over 52 percent of the overall school population, making our school "racially imbalanced." School district officials wanted to keep the enrollment of Black students to "no less than 15 percent and no more than 45 percent." This was a mandate by the New York State Education Department. Really, without anyone saying so, the goal was always to have Black students in the minority. Even if the school reached the highest number of Black students it could have—45 percent—Black students would never be the majority. Black families would never be in the majority. I attended a school that was, according to the district and state goals, imbalanced because Black kids and their families were the majority.

44

The Black student population continued to grow in my home city. It wasn't until 1992 (fifteen years after the state mandate and thirty-eight years after *Brown v. Board of Education*) that the school district adopted a new policy around integration and racial balance in schools. This policy stated that all the schools in the district should stay within 20 percent of the average number of minority students. This meant that each school could possibly have between 20 and 70 percent Black and Brown students, so for once, they could be in the majority.

As a society, we never really gave school integration a solid chance. The government (both federal and state) and school officials spent time and resources on creating short-term solutions with unrealistic goals. They didn't work to establish a sustainable and equitable desegregation program, and school integration was abandoned at its peak.

Decision-makers with power wanted a quick fix to a very big problem that still persists today, affecting our lives historically,

PRE-1992 LIMIT ON THE ENROLLMENT OF BLACK STUDENTS

NY STATE EDUCATION MANDATE

15-45% BLACK STUDENTS

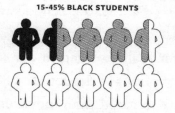

55-85% WHITE STUDENTS

TIFFANY'S SCHOOL

52% BLACK STUDENTS

48% WHITE STUDENTS

POST-1992 LIMIT ON THE ENROLLMENT OF BLACK STUDENTS

20-70% BLACK & BROWN STUDENTS

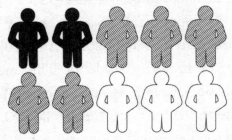

economically, socially, culturally, and morally. School segregation isn't just a school problem—it never was. The issue of our deeply segregated schools was really about our segregated neighborhoods, and that was rarely, if ever, addressed.

The building of Interstate 81 in the late 1950s guaranteed that some of my city's neighborhoods would be stuck in a highway underpass in a valley or trapped north or south of downtown. The highway was the way out for many White middle-class families. It carried them to the suburbs, where the yards were bigger, and the schools were better funded. It carried them away, leaving those of us with fewer resources behind. Because our neighborhoods were so divided, our schools were, by extension, divided and unequal.

School-integration efforts never really worked in our midsize city. They didn't work in a lot of places in the country. Since 1990, schools have become more segregated than they were in the early 1960s. And the problem is worse in the Northeast and the Midwest, despite the continued belief that this is solely a Southern problem. School integration never really worked because it was never about desegregating neighborhoods. It was about creating a visibly equal population of students in schools. The school-integration efforts of districts across the country were at their best in the late 1980s. This was also around the time when there was the smallest academic gap between Black students and White students.

Education advocates, administrators, and districts shifted the focus from integrating schools to closing the achievement gap. Multiple presidential administrations and district officials have talked about how to close the gaps without addressing why the gaps exist in the first place. They've done this for years. What they don't typically acknowledge is that the gaps they talk about exist between students and that racial, ethnic, and class lines are better understood when we address intersectionality and confront segregation that exists in our communities and schools.

I want to pause here for a moment and talk about what is known as the **ACHIEVEMENT GAP**.

The achievement gap is a phrase that is often used when people discuss the difference between White affluent students and students who are historically marginalized and exploited. (This includes students of the Global Majority, students who are poor or living in poverty, students whose first language is not English, students with disabilities, and so on.) The difference is often explained as a gap in academic achievement between students. The gap is usually measured by the differences in test scores between Black and Latine students and White students.

Some schools and districts have shifted to using the phrase **OPPORTUNITY GAP**. This subtle change in words helps explain how and why some students have many opportunities to succeed in school settings and others do not. The opportunity gap looks at the obstacles students face in school and that may make it difficult for them to have the same kind of success the classmates of the dominant culture have.

While the achievement gap blames people for the inability to be successful in school (whether that's due to inheritance, culture, or something else), the term opportunity gap shifts the blame to conditions in society.

However, instead of using either of the terms, I prefer to use what critical-race-theory scholar Gloria Ladson-Billings refers to as the "education debt." This is the debt that is owed to students of the Global Majority, a debt that has grown over decades and centuries. As Gloria Ladson-Billings says, "The historical, economic, sociopolitical, and moral decisions and policies that characterize our society have created an education debt."

For hundreds and hundreds of years, Black people, Indigenous people, and People of the Global Majority have been purposely, systematically, and systemically excluded from education and learning. We've also been excluded from holding positions in government and having decision-making power. Schools have been consistently funded differently and inequitably depending on where they are and who makes up their student populations.

Our schools were segregated because our neighborhoods were. We were divided by our racialized and ethnic backgrounds and were separated by economic status and class.

My home city, like many others, tried to integrate schools

THE HISTORICAL ECONOMIC SOCIOPOLITICAL AND MORAL DECISIONS AND POLICIES THAT CHARACTERIZE OUR SOCIETY HAVE CREATED AN EDUCATION DEBT

- DR. GLORIA LADSON-BILLINGS

in the early 1960s, but it didn't work. District officials made decisions behind closed doors. They allowed a few of the most vocal White caregivers to sway their decisions and ended up closing some of the only schools where Black students were in the majority.

If the schools where all the Black kids go are closed, where do they go? They'll have to go to other schools, right? Black students were displaced and forced to transfer to schools where most of the students and teachers were White. This was not a situation that was unique to my home city. This happened all over the country. Our district, like many others, was seeking more racially balanced schools. School-board members and district administrators didn't include the input of members of the community in the planning and decision-making. They may have listened to a few of the White caregivers, but they didn't hear the many Black and Brown caregivers and students. The solutions they did come up with were rolled out in bits and pieces.

School integration never worked in my home city because the district failed to address the root causes of our divide. They looked for quick fixes, like implementing school choice by way of shutting down schools, implementing busing, and introducing magnet schools. The onus was on children to bear the brunt of integrating the city and fixing the problem of segregation. Again, this is not unique to Syracuse. This happened in cities and towns all over the country. This happened in your city and in your state.

ROBERTO

The Discipline Problem

By Roberto Germán

Long nights
Hands covering my ears
Thinking it's gon' stop me from hearing my fighting parents
    forcing divorce into
The picture
Then give off the appearance in the morning that they're still
    married

No hot meal today
No, sir, no, ma'am
We're in a rush
Gon' have to eat school breakfast and lunch

Searching for a hat, jacket, and backpack
Already fifteen minutes late
Car line's ridiculous
Get out here!
No warm embrace
Late ticket at the gate
Stale, bootleg Frosted Flakes for breakfast
Man, I can't catch a break!

But I can't clearly articulate how I'm feeling
So I clench my fist and start screaming!
Staring at you like, Really?
When you ask, "How are you doing today?"

Shoulder shrug

Of course I care
Just in another world like an open stare
Until my head's down
'Cause I don't want to look around with these teary eyes
Hard for me to trust when I feel like everyone I know is feeding
    me lies

Yet I'm hungry and since I was acting up, I missed snack time
Veggie sticks and hummus
Oh, how I so wanted some veggie sticks and hummus!
Now I won't stop humming
H hmmm hmmmmm, hmmmmm hmm hmmmmm
H hmmm hmmmmm, hmmmmm hmm hmmmmm

My not-so-quiet voice disrupted the work cycle
Materials hit the floor
Peers trying to ignore me but my behaviors are far from boring
And now that I have your ATTENTION . . .
I've been removed from the class
Told I could reenter the community when I am ready but . . .
Who knows how long this will last

I didn't mean any harm
Why am I so bad?
Fetal position
I'm in my feelings
Internalizing my poor choices
Hearing a voice that is offering a working definition of who I
    am . . .
The Discipline Problem

This piece was inspired by my experience with early-elementary students several years ago. This particular child was one of my often-disciplined students. She was a Black girl from a single-parent household. She was strong, smart, and talented. She also demonstrated challenging behaviors for a host of different reasons, including the classroom environment.

I tried to reach this child in many ways. However, if I am honest with myself, I harmed her more than I helped her. I still feel a sense of disappointment. I allowed my growing frustrations and my bias to blur the way I viewed her. There were too many occasions in which my response to her behaviors reinforced the very things I was training our guides *not* to do. Guilty as charged! I wish my learning and growth did not come at her expense or other students' that experienced the same thing from me at some point in time. Yet I know there are tapes playing in my mind that require dismantling so that I can lovingly approach each student in the fullness of who they are.

There is much that I have learned and relearned since then. Sometimes we need to be exposed to new information and strategies. Sometimes we simply need to be reminded about best practices. Sometimes we just need to hold up a mirror and hold ourselves accountable. To the extent that I am able to, I try to proactively meet with students and families with the goal of establishing a connection that will be continually fostered throughout the school year. It's also been helpful to go beyond their racial and ethnic culture and learn about their home culture. This has broadened my understanding of the students and families and deters me from making harmful and biased assumptions.

WHAT I LEARNED ABOUT ELEMENTARY SCHOOL

My preschool classroom was in a trailer. It was a temporary structure on the school grounds, but it was ours. One corner held shelves filled with wooden blocks of various lengths. Our paintings adorned the walls. The sink actually felt reachable for my three-year-old self. We sat on the floor and at tables where we chatted with our friends in our little voices. I loved both my preschool teachers and our classroom. One of my teachers was a grandmother who rode a motorcycle on the weekends, and the other had rosy cheeks and an asymmetric haircut. There, we got to be kids and do the things that kids do.

Later, in kindergarten, I learned how to dance like a 1920s flapper from my friend. I learned that my teacher didn't know what to say when I told her my dad got in a car accident and was in a coma. (She just walked away and continued passing out whatever worksheets we were coloring that day.) I learned that I had to play with the boy who looked up girls' skirts and got in the most trouble because my teacher thought I could help keep him out of trouble. (Maybe she needed a break, but she shouldn't have put that on me—a five-year-old.)

I went to one of the worst schools in the state, according to the New York State Education Department. There were two in our city district, my elementary school and one on the north side. That was the same year I learned how to take the state tests and use my no. 2 pencil to fill out the Scantron sheets. Those tests determined if my classmates and I went to a "deficient" school. How we performed on those tests determined whether our school would stay open. Test scores defined our school, but they didn't define us.

I learned that which reading group you got placed into mattered. I learned how to stop saying the Pledge of Allegiance and how to build an imaginary brick wall around my desk when I wanted to concentrate or escape. I learned that it was okay for my teacher to regularly misspell words and control when we could go to the restroom. I learned that it was okay for her to talk about how great her own White children were in their suburban school, that they got to meet Bruce Coville, while all we got was her reading *My Teacher Is an Alien* to us. I learned that, no matter how inviting the classroom looked, you might not feel safe inside the space. I learned that the adults made up the rules, and if we didn't follow them, we'd have to put our heads down or write the same sentence over and over again, a sentence that felt like a coerced admission of guilt rather than a support

55

to help us do better next time. I learned that it was okay for my teacher to call us names and make racist remarks because she continued to be our teacher and we had no recourse.

But in second grade, I had a teacher who loved us. Every day she showed us she loved us by keeping us close. She didn't send kids out of the classroom. She trusted us.

Third grade felt like a turning point, the year I turned from being a wholehearted optimist who saw good in everyone and everything to a kid who kept an internal list of questions, trying to figure out all the strange and unjust nuances of my little world.

My fourth-grade classroom sat just a few doors down from the ISS (in-school suspension), room and the cafeteria food smells wafted our way each day. That was the year we learned about local history and government. I remember learning about the Onondaga and the Haudenosaunee. We learned about wampum and longhouses. But we didn't learn about the Great Law of Peace. We didn't learn that the Onondaga people are still very much alive. We didn't learn that we were on their stolen land.

Elementary school was where I learned I wasn't White and I wasn't Black, that I was "other." It's where all my teachers looked like a few of my classmates but not the majority of us. Officer Friendly made frequent visits (until we got too old to be cute). Drug Abuse Resistance Education (DARE for short) convinced me never to use drugs, and it was in that program that I learned that the cops thought it was cool to confiscate drug dealers' cars and slap the DARE logo on them.

My fifth-grade teacher taught us that, at the time, our Onondaga Lake was the most polluted lake in the country. We read *A Wrinkle in Time* in our math group and discussed the possibility of a fifth dimension.

Sixth grade was the year I learned that some of the adults with power believed I was exceptional, that I could be more deserving than my classmates and schoolmates. A few of us, instead of going to our usual classrooms Monday mornings, were picked up by a yellow bus that carried us away to the gifted and talented program, located in another building. There, a bunch of other talented and gifted—and more White than I was used to—sixth graders from the other city elementary schools got together to paint frescoes, participate in a mock trial, sit on couches rather than at desks, build and launch rockets, and take machines apart just for the sake of taking them apart. We were a select few from within our district. We were smart. We were remarkable. In truth, we were no better than anyone else in our district, but hopping on that yellow bus to learn in a different kind of way told us otherwise.

MINH

Self(less) Portrait: A Kind of One-Act Play

By Minh Lê

Narrator (present–day Minh): Before we begin, let's take a look at this picture.

Here we have a young boy (me) standing in front of a self-portrait that was chosen for a district-wide art show. It's not exactly the greatest work of art ever, but we're not here as art critics. No, we're more interested in the boy himself. If we look closely, we'll see that his smile is strangely hesitant and he has the slightest hint of mischief in his eyes, almost as if he's holding a secret.

Well, guess what—he *does* have a secret, but to find out what it is, we'll have to travel all the way back to third grade . . .

Setting (Flashback): The year is 1987. We open up on a third-grade art class in suburban Connecticut. Children sit in small groups around dark brown pentagon-shaped tables. The art teacher walks around the room with a box of small circular mirrors. She places a handful on each table.

Teacher: Today's assignment is "Self-Portraits." I want every-one to take one of these mirrors and look at yourselves as you draw. Try to pay close attention to details and really put yourself on the page.

The teacher leaves several mirrors on a table where young Minh and other students are sitting. The kids grab for the mir-rors and realize that there aren't enough to go around. One kid raises a hand to get the teacher's attention, but young Minh stops them.

Kid 1: Mrs.—
Minh: Wait.

Minh and his friend (the only other Asian American boy in the room) look at each other. They smile knowingly.

Minh and friend: We don't need mirrors . . . we'll just draw each other!

Having resolved the situation, the students start on their assignment. Most of the kids look into their personal mirrors as they draw, while the two Asian American students draw each other.

End scene

Narrator (me again, back in the present): So, what was the secret behind young Minh's smile?

That's not him in his self-portrait.

There's a lot for us to unpack here. At the time, this portrait swap just felt like a clever solution to a simple problem, but looking back, it says a lot about what happens when you don't see yourself represented or reflected at school. To understand that better, let's talk a little more about mirrors.

Today I get to write books for children, and something that's discussed a lot in the publishing world is the importance of books as mirrors for readers, especially children (shout-out to the legend Dr. Rudine Sims Bishop). By mirror books, I mean books where you can see parts of yourself and your life within their pages. Books as mirrors can be important and affirming because it is a chance to see yourself reflected back and validated by a story.

For the young Minh in this picture, while he didn't have a literal mirror in art class, he also didn't have many metaphorical mirrors in the books around him. And many of the mirror books that did exist were distorted reflections that showed Asians and Asian Americans as either sidekicks or stereotypes. In fact, at the time, the most prominent book featuring Asian characters was *The Five Chinese Brothers,* which has all kinds of problems, including racist illustrations and the premise that no one could tell these five Chinese characters apart (which reinforced the heinous and pervasive "all Asians look alike" stereotype).

It's easy for children to internalize the messages in these books, so it's not surprising that my friend and I thought drawing a picture of each other would be close enough for a self-portrait. We were the only two Asian American boys in class, so people always lumped us together and often mistook my friend and me for each other. I felt that people were unable to see the differences between us, and eventually I started to see things that way too.

Things have (thankfully) changed a lot since the 1980s, but there is still a long way to go. There is a more diverse selection of books available now, and you all deserve to be surrounded by nuanced and reaffirming reflections of yourselves in your books, in your schools, in your everyday life. I hope that you all have access to as many mirrors as you could possibly want, mirrors that reflect the full range of yourself: the serious,

61

the silly, and everything in between. And when it comes to your self-image, unlike me, never settle for close enough . . . because you should never have to look at a self-portrait and see someone else smiling back at you.

EMMANUEL

Emmanuel's Story

By Emmanuel

When I was in elementary school, a student in my class took some candy without asking and shared it with me and some of my friends. Some of my friends were Black and the student who took the candy was white. When we were in the hall walking back to the classroom, my teacher, who was white, made me and my Black friends stand in a separate line from all our other classmates. She made us walk down the hall, and when other adults walked by us, she told them that we were in this line because we took something that wasn't ours. When we got to the classroom, she made us turn out our pockets, and she checked our backpacks in front of the rest of the students. I was furious. After all the Black students had gotten in trouble, my white friend finally told the teacher that he was the one who had taken the candy and shared it. I was not mad at my friend because he had been scared of telling the truth. I was very mad at my teacher for making a big problem out of a small problem.

We were little kids and it felt like she cared more about the piece of candy that was missing than about the Black children that she thought had taken it.

I felt lucky to go to school with Black students. But I had only had one Brown teacher. I was in middle school, and I really hoped that I'd have at least one Black teacher every year. Even if the Black teachers were very hard or strict, I thought they would understand how to treat children respectfully and care for us.

JAMES

What I've Learned About Racism

By James Bird

What I've learned about racism is that it doesn't always come at you swinging fists and spitting out slurs. It's not always violent and loud. Sometimes, racism comes at you smiling.

When I was ten, I was the only Native American kid in my Sunday-school class. I was not Christian, but my mom thought attending Sunday school was a good way for me to make friends and be in a safe place while she was at work. So every Sunday, she'd take me on the bus from Tustin, California, to a city called Irvine to spend the day with all the other kids. And all the other kids were white, but when you're young, things like skin color don't matter at all. Toys are everything.

One day, a boy from class had a birthday party. Everyone was invited—even me. This boy had the best toys and always wore clothes that looked brand-new. I, however, grew up very poor and often had to repeat my outfits. Many times, we were evicted from our apartment and had to live in our red Pinto for a week or two. And some of those times, my mom parked in the lot of that same church where I attended Sunday school. I never had new toys or new clothes, but I begged and begged my mom to get this kid a birthday present. I didn't want to be the one kid who showed up empty-handed.

Even though we had no money for toys, we took the bus to the local mall, and I picked out the coolest present I could find: a can full of bendable musclemen. It felt so cool to hold it in my hands. I wanted it so badly. This kid was so lucky to get this present.

After my mom paid for the toy, we took the bus to the kid's house. I wore my best shirt and pants, and my mom even wore a dress. The entire bus ride felt like an adventure. We headed into this beautiful upscale land full of green trees, huge lawns, and mansions. I'd never seen anything like it before. This was the kind of place where kids grew up having both parents, and each parent had a car. This was the kind of place where kids had their own rooms. It was vastly different from what I knew. I shared a room with my sister and brother, and that's when we even had a room to share.

We got off the bus, and as we walked a few blocks into the residential neighborhood, I felt like I was in a movie. There was house after house. Garden after garden. The street was so clean. There were no homeless people sitting on the curbs. There were no police cars patrolling up and down the block. And not one house had bars over its windows. I imagined this was the heaven that Sunday school taught us about.

When we reached the address, there were a dozen balloons tied along the white picket fence surrounding the gigantic two-story house. Music was blasting, and no neighbors were complaining. And there must have been twenty cars lined up on one side of the street. This kid must be very popular.

My mom and I entered the home. It seemed even bigger inside. There were mothers sipping from wineglasses in a kitchen that was larger than our entire apartment. There were fathers huddled on a couch in the living room watching football on a TV that was almost as large as the wall behind it. I was in awe. But the best part was the overflowing pile of wrapped gifts that engulfed the table. There were so many. More than all the presents I'd ever gotten in my ten years of living.

I didn't even care that my gift for this boy was the smallest. I knew how great it was. It would probably be his favorite present. I knew it would have been mine. I placed it on the top of the gift pile proudly. The boy's mother greeted my mom and me and told us to make ourselves at home. But that was impossible. There were no cockroaches here. There were no cracks in the walls, and there definitely were no parts of the carpet you had to avoid because the floorboards were rotting underneath it.

My mom asked to use the restroom, because it had been a long bus ride, and the boy's mother walked my mom to it. I stood there alone. The kids were all playing in the backyard, but I was too shy to join them. I decided to wait for my mom, so I took a seat in the hall. When my mom came out, we didn't head to the back with the rest of the kids; instead, I followed my mom to the kitchen. And before we went in, we heard all the mothers gossiping. My mom stopped. Her body went kinda stiff from

67

hearing something she didn't like. I stepped forward to hear, and my body kinda went stiff too. The boy's mother tried to whisper, but her quiet voice was as loud as a regular voice. She told the other mothers to keep an eye on me and my mom. She mentioned that we were poor Indians and had nothing and that I attended Sunday school only so we could keep our car parked in the church parking lot. Indians steal, she said. Keep an eye on them, she said.

I was a kid. Her words just confused me. They didn't hurt me the way I could see from my mom's face they had hurt her. My mom took my hand, and we entered the kitchen. The boy's mom immediately stopped talking and put on her best smile. My mom thanked her for the invitation and told her we had to go. The boy's mom pretended to frown; so did all the other mothers there. Then my mom told me to go to the present table and get my gift. "That kid has enough toys. Today is his day, but it's also your day. Every day is your day—never forget that," my mom said. I was so excited. I grabbed the gift, and we left the house. The entire walk back to the bus stop felt strange. My mom was mad. So mad. But I was happy. So happy. I couldn't wait to get home and open this present.

I said earlier what I've learned about racism is that it doesn't always come at you with anger and hate, that it sometimes comes at you with a smile, because that boy's mom always seemed so nice to me. She was always smiling at me in class. Maybe I should have mentioned it earlier, but that boy's mom was my Sunday-school teacher.

WHAT I LEARNED ABOUT HATCHET

This part of my school story happened when I was in sixth grade. It took place inside the sandy-brown-colored school that occupied more than half the block on the south side. The group of kids in this story had been on each floor, in many of the classrooms, the library, and the cafeteria, part of which doubled as the gym. We had all gone to this school for most of our young lives.

We were in a classroom that was not actually a typical classroom; it was the reading-resource room. There was a big wooden table in the middle of the room. Wooden chairs surrounded that table. There was a big green movable chalkboard that helped partition the room into different, smaller learning areas. It was a shared room on the first floor of the school.

I was one of the kids in this story. Most of us had known each other for a long time, since at least first grade. Most of us lived in the neighborhood. We had all been given labels like *advanced*

69

reader, above average, gifted and talented, or all of the above. Our school administrators and even some of our teachers saw us as extraordinary and special. We were smart kids, according to the grades we got on our assignments and our state test scores.

And then there was our teacher. She was a nice White lady. She wore long khaki skirts and sweaters, and her white hair was cut in a practical short do. From what I remember, our teacher was pretty new to the school's community. I didn't really know anything about her; she never shared much about herself with us. I didn't even know whether she lived in our city or not. She enthusiastically over-assigned acrostic poetry, though. There were so many acrostic poems written that year. She didn't know much about us either. She knew our PEP and Iowa Test scores. She knew our labels. She knew our reading levels. And she knew our names. That was about it.

This story is about our reading group and the book *Hatchet*. Published in 1986, *Hatchet* by Gary Paulsen won the John Newbery Medal in 1988 along with many other awards.

I have a feeling many of you already know about *Hatchet*. Some of you have probably read it too. In case you haven't read it and you don't know what it's about, I'll summarize it for you in three short sentences:

It's about a White boy named Brian.

Following a traumatic plane crash, Brian is stranded and lost in the Canadian wilderness for over fifty days and learns how to survive.

Thankfully, Brian has the hatchet his mother gave him.

Our small group of advanced readers was tasked with reading and discussing *Hatchet*. Our teacher was excited to share the book with our group. We were not equally excited to read it.

Most of us had no idea what a hatchet was. I'm pretty sure not one of us had ever held one or even seen one. Some of us had never even heard of such a thing. (I was one of them. *Wasn't a hatchet just an ax?* It was a complete unknown to me.)

The only thing that was relatable was being cold, but Brian, the White boy in the book, wasn't even *that* cold because he was stranded during the summer.

In general, we did not like the book. To this day, some of us dislike it so much that the word *hate* comes up. (Me again.)

Unfortunately, and typically, this school story doesn't really have a point. It doesn't have a resolution. It doesn't even have an end. It just kind of keeps going, getting passed down from one year to the next, going from one school to another, from one teacher to another, and so on. The groups of kids change, the school settings change (slightly), but *Hatchet* is a bestseller even now, which means it's still being assigned to a lot of kids, probably a lot of kids like our group of sixth graders.

Hatchet was one of the worst books our teacher could have assigned us—and I'm not exaggerating.

We, a group of Black and Brown kids, working-class and poor kids, city kids whose lives spanned a few blocks (including our own school); if our world needed to expand beyond our blocks, we could get there by taking the bus. We, a group of kids who endured years of microaggressions and macroaggressions and all the general aggressions in between. We, a group of kids who had to smile at Officer Friendly, a person who didn't care to know our names or our faces once he turned his back and walked out of our classrooms.

We.

We, a group of kids who were smart and brave and no more special than any of the other kids who were not invited to that big brown table. Not exceptional. We, a group of kids who found *Hatchet* to be just as boring and pointless as the endless acrostic assignments. We didn't need to read a book about a White boy learning how to survive in an unknown environment. We already knew how to survive. We needed to read books about people like us. We needed to see ourselves and our future greatness reflected to us.

Our teacher meant no harm. In fact, she probably thought she was doing a lot of good in our city school. When she told people about her job, she probably prefaced it by saying, "I work in a Title One school." I think she genuinely liked us, or at least she thought we were all right. However, she didn't know us. She didn't even try to get to know us. She didn't see us. She didn't hear us. We were just props in her do-good teaching story.

Our teacher spent so much time trying to contain our words with acrostics and our dreams with unrelatable stories that we could never be a part of when what we really needed was for our teacher to go beyond herself, to go beyond the stereotypes she believed to be true.

We needed not just to see ourselves in the books we read. We needed to know that we were limitless. We needed our voices, our thoughts, our creativity, and our joy to be welcomed.

We needed our teacher to center us.

We needed her to see our value and know our worth.

We needed to know that there was humanity in us too, that we, like the White boy in *Hatchet*, had the capacity not only to survive but to grow into mature, compassionate human beings . . . because we did. And not because of her.

I like to imagine what that class might have been like if our teacher in her khaki skirts and sweaters had shared some of her power with us, if she had shifted beyond the status quo and her socially constructed expectations of us and for us . . . if she had realized that we had just as much to teach her as she had to teach us. How great our lessons and our discussions could have been.

What if she had imagined a new purpose for that table we sat around? And in the middle of it rested us and our community and our voices and our thoughts and our experiences?

What if *our* stories were at the center of that table, of our learning?

What if she had put forth, on that big brown table, all the possibilities rather than her limits for us?

MY
MIDD
SCH

LE

HOOL

MY MIDDLE SCHOOL

Middle school (or, as we called it when I was there, junior high) was the next stop in my schooling journey, and it was where multiple elementary schools converged. We rode city buses with drivers who would rather not shuttle young teenagers to and from school. I went to the same junior high my mom and her siblings went to. It was our neighborhood school. A portrait of the guy the school was named after greeted us in the foyer. None of us who entered the building knew who he was or what he'd done. The building structure itself was nothing special; it was only one story high, surrounded by small green fields and parking lots. There was a creek behind the back fields, and a small bridge connected one of the neighborhoods to the school. A different field in a different direction ended at the back of the local branch of the library, another at the ice-skating rink.

Years before I even started my schooling journey, more than a quarter of the city's Black middle-school students attended this junior high. The community's identity changed quickly and some of the White families in the neighborhood did not like that. They were very vocal about the change in student demographics, and that scared the school board. One of the White caregivers told the school board at the time, "The school is getting a reputation from police, teachers, and kids that it is a totally Black school." The board members were afraid the White families would bail and go to other, predominantly White, public schools in the city or to private schools. That year, in hopes of reducing the 58 percent Black student population, the school board capped the enrollment of Black students, something they'd never done before. Only Black seventh graders were admitted, and they closed admissions to Black eighth graders. Within a month of the cap, the population of Black students dropped by 3 percent. Two years later, the population of Black students dropped to less than 44 percent, ensuring Black students wouldn't be in the majority at the school. By the time I entered the halls, the cap had been lifted, and the district's and state's racial-balance goals had changed.

On the outside, our junior high looked integrated. You could see it when all the students waited to enter the building each morning. The school looked like the product of a successful integration experiment. But on the inside, things were different. The school was very segregated. Some classrooms were

77

filled with nearly all White students. Some classes were filled with nearly all Black and Brown students. Not a lot of classes had a "racial balance." It felt very different from elementary school . . . too different.

LORENA

What I Remember (Part One)

By Lorena Germán

I remember in seventh grade one of my teachers, Mrs. Y., did a terrible thing. My classmate was reading aloud. Slowly. Struggling through the lines. Working his way through. Making gains. And doing it in front of all of us. You know what Mrs. Y. did? She blurted out, as he walked through the letters and words, "If you were half as fast reading as you were on the court, we would have been done by now. My God!" This was in liberal, progressive, nonracist, bastion-of-freedom Massachusetts.

And later, after my head cold evolved into an acute sinus infection, then bronchitis, and then pneumonia (that affects my respiratory system to this day) and I had missed twelve days of school and was simply trying to return and get the basics done, she said, "She's just not the same anymore." And my mother, though angry, begged, "She was very sick at home. She had pneumonia. Please, give her a chance." Her stubbornness wasn't lost on me, nor was it a surprise. What she didn't know was that doctors weren't really supporting me and so it took me longer to recover. Finally, a Dominican family friend who was also a doctor came over and checked me in the middle of one of my highest fevers, and it was his recommendations and prescriptions that led me to heal.

WHAT I LEARNED ABOUT TRACKING

It's Monday morning.

You and your friends wait outside the school building with the rest of your classmates.

The bell alerts you. You and everyone else slowly head toward the building.

You are about to start another school day.

Every day starts the same way.

You enter through the front doors and take a left. You pass by the front office. You keep going until you are at an intersection of hallways.

You have a choice:

You take a right and head into the hall that is in the back of the school. If you do this, you are a Team Three kid.

You stay fairly straight and go into the hall in the middle of this school wing. If you do this, you are a Team Two kid.

You veer left and enter the hall in the front of the school. If you do this, you are a Team One kid.

***

You are a Team Three kid. You greet the hall monitor, who has a seat in the corner. Your locker is located at the end of the hall near your science class, and you pass by other students who are putting their things away into their lockers. Teachers stand in their doorways. They watch you and your peers.

You settle into your English class. It's your first one of the day. A couple of your friends are in the class too, but your teacher has assigned your seats so none of you are sitting near one another. Most of the other students in your class are familiar to you. They're Black and Brown kids who went to the same elementary school as you. A red English and grammar textbook is waiting for you at your seat. Your teacher has written the assignment on the board. Every day starts the same. You spend about ten or fifteen minutes silently editing sentences and paragraphs to make them grammatically correct. It reminds you of the work you did in fourth grade.

Your teacher sits at the desk in the front of the room, taking attendance. There's a stack of paperback books on the desk. You'll be starting a new read today.

One of your classmates comes in late. They look out of breath and slip into their seat in the third row.

"You're late." Without looking up, your teacher holds out a hand, waiting for the late pass.

Your classmate tells the teacher they don't have one. They

start to open up the grammar book, but your teacher tells them to go get a pass before they settle in. Your classmate starts to tell the teacher the bus was late and one of the hall monitors told everyone to just get to class. The teacher says, "Go to the office and don't come back until you have a pass."

Your classmate grabs their backpack and leaves class, leaving the door open. You can hear the hall monitor ask them why they're leaving class.

You have a hard time getting back to work and don't finish the grammar assignment. It'll be part of your homework now.

The rest of your day isn't much different. You have math and science classes. You have PE and computer lab. Throughout the day, the hall monitors do just that—monitor the hallways and make sure you and your classmates are getting where you need to go and quickly. The bell rings at the end of class; you grab your things from your locker. You and your friends make a plan to meet outside. The hall monitors walk down the hall reminding everyone to get a move on, school has ended.

***

You are a Team Two kid. You find your locker. One of your teachers is standing in their doorway, greeting you and the other students as you walk by. Another, at the end of the corridor, watches over the hall. Some of the doors are still closed. Your locker is right next to your social studies class.

You settle into your English class. It's the first one of the day. A couple of your friends are in the class too, but your teacher has assigned your seats and you get to sit near only one of them.

83

There is a writing prompt on the board. Your teacher asks everyone to read the prompt and start planning your writing while they take attendance. You say "Here" or "Present" when your name is called. A couple of your classmates aren't here yet.

Every Monday starts with a writing prompt. You spend the first half of this class writing, editing, and finishing up a piece based on the prompt. The assignments are repetitive, but they're not bad.

After everyone has been writing for twenty minutes, the teacher says you'll spend the rest of the class watching the old *Romeo and Juliet* movie that you started last week after reading the play. You didn't totally understand the language in the play, and the film seems old and dated, but seeing the actions in the movie helps.

One of your classmates comes in late. They look out of breath and slip into their seat in the third row.

Your teacher looks up and gestures for your classmate to come to the desk. They talk quietly. You hear your classmate tell your teacher the bus was late and no one was given a late pass. Your teacher tells them to return to their desk and that they'll check in with the office later.

Your classmate starts the writing prompt. You return to your work.

The rest of your day isn't much different. You have math and science classes. You have music and Spanish classes. The hall monitor doesn't pay much attention to you and your classmates until the end of the day. The monitors spend most of their time in the Team Three hall and near the cafeteria. The bell rings at the end of class; you grab your things from your locker and wait for your friends. The roaming hall monitor tells you to move along and meet your friends outside.

***

You are a Team One kid. You shield your eyes because the sunlight in the hall is so bright. Your locker is located outside your English class. All of the classroom doors are open. You pass a couple of classmates who are passing a soccer ball back and forth and you try to avoid tripping. You notice a couple of your teachers in a classroom together. No one comes out to tell the kids to put the soccer ball in a locker.

You settle into your English class. It's the first one of the day. A couple of your friends are in the class too. You are one of a few kids of the Global Majority in the class. Most of your other classmates are White and went to a different elementary school than you. During the first week of school, your teacher let you choose where you wanted to sit and now you sit next to and in front of your closest friends. The week's assignments are on the board. Usually, you start the day silently reading a short story or the book your class is covering, but today is a little different.

Your teacher comes in when everyone is seated and reminds you you're going on a field trip soon, then takes attendance. You say "Here" when your name is called.

Your teacher goes over the field-trip plan and guidelines. It's a whole-day trip. You'll be back in time for dismissal. All the Team One kids are going on the same field trip this the week,

85

and Monday is your class's turn. You're going for a ride on a boat along the Erie Canal. The field trip doesn't really relate to any of the things you've been learning in your classes, but it'll be fun.

Your teacher tells your class you have some free time (about twenty minutes) to read or write. Your choice.

One of your classmates comes in late, just as you're about to pack up and head out to the school bus. They look out of breath and slip into their seat in the third row.

Your teacher smiles at them and remarks they made it just in time. They then ask everyone to ready themselves for the field trip. You board the bus with the rest of your classmates.

You and your classmates return to school at the end of the day. You've missed your math and science classes. You missed PE, but you have about thirty minutes left of your Spanish class. Your teacher plays a video about México City, pausing it to tell you stories from their childhood. The bell rings at the end of class; you grab your things from your locker and wait for your friends, then you all walk out of the building together.

***

But the thing is, even if you wanted to choose your own middle-school adventure, you couldn't. It was already chosen for you.

You don't know how anyone ends up a Team One, Team Two, or Team Three kid. It's something you're ushered into on the first day of school and it stays with you throughout your whole middle-school experience.

I was a Team One kid, veering left every morning. The hall that was home to Team One was where my homeroom and most of my classes were.

I wasn't on a team in elementary school. There, all of the sixth-grade classes were in the same hall, all of the first-grade classes were together, and so on. But in middle school, there was no seventh-grade hallway; everything seemed to be all mixed up. Math and English classes were right next to each other. Seventh and eighth graders shared some of the same spaces. I was a Team One kid during both of my middle-school years. My team status never changed.

I don't know how I ended up a Team One kid. A few of my friends and classmates from elementary school had lockers near mine in the first hallway, but others, most of them, were scattered and on other teams. Many of the other kids on my team were from different elementary schools. Most of them were White and lived in homes their families owned and with both of their parents. Specials classes, PE, and lunch were all with the Team One kids and I didn't see many of the other kids at my school until the end of the day.

I met new people during my first days of middle school. I saw some of my old friends, but most of the people in my Team One classes were unfamiliar. Many of them already knew each other. A lot of them went to the same elementary school. I met a couple of the kids from the gifted and talented program I was in the year before. They become my lifeline and my friends. They introduced me to their friends, and I soon became folded into a new group of people who mostly did not look like me. They looked more like the people I watched on television and characters from the books I read. I started to lose touch with my old schoolmates even though we were all in the same building at the same time. Even though our school looked diverse from the outside, the classrooms felt (and were) much more segregated than any classes I had ever experienced before.

***

I felt so separated from the other kids in my school; even my twin was a Team Two kid. My middle–school life revolved around the Team One hallway and my new Team One (White) friends. I worked on the school yearbook, ran on the track team, and became a peer leader. I went to sleepovers and spent weekends hanging out at the mall. I immersed myself in the culture of *My So-Called Life* and *Friends*. Thankfully, *Sister, Sister* was still there to show me some reflection of who I was. I wore oversize flannel shirts and tried to control and hide the natural curl in my hair. I crushed on Team One White boys who played lacrosse, watched *Beavis and Butt-Head*, and liked White girls. I tried to blend in. I imagined myself as a character in my own life story, but not the main character. I could never be the main character—not yet, anyway. I wanted to believe I belonged, and my Team One status affirmed that for me. And it also confused me.

Our Team One teachers had high expectations for us. They didn't try to manage our bodies. They encouraged discussion. And even though we were thirteen, we were already on track to go to college. Our team felt like the best team. It went without saying. We got to go on a lot of field trips that none of the other teams did. Believe it or not, we even had the brightest hallway in the school—it felt like the light shone on us because we were the ones who deserved it the most. That same light coming in from the windows shone on me and affirmed that my Team One status meant that I could be exceptional.

I want to pause here for a moment and explain what the teams actually were.

Imagine you're getting ready to run around a racetrack. Typically, regardless of where you start—the inner lane, somewhere in the middle, or the outermost lane of the track—you and the other racers have an equal distance to run. The starting positions are staggered so the length around is the same for everyone. But this isn't the same when it comes to academics. There's no staggered start in schooling.

My team, Team One, started at the innermost lane; we had the shortest distance to travel around the track and we were guaranteed to win any race we took part in. We had the high expectations of our teachers and counselors. We had the advanced courses that propelled us into the college-preparatory route in high school and beyond. We took our state Regents exams and passed them. We had the care and trust of the school and the community to go forth and be great.

This wasn't the same for the other teams, though. The farther back you went in the school, the darker the halls became (at least, it seemed that way). Students who were funneled into Teams Two and Three were not treated the same as Team One students. Advanced classes did not exist for the other teams. Some of the Team Two students, like my sister and some of our friends, took classes in the Team One hallway with mostly Team One kids, but that wasn't true for everyone. The other teams didn't go on nearly as many field trips as we did. Their teachers didn't hold the same high expectations for them either. More Team Three kids than Team One kids were in detention and suspended.

The different hallways, the different classes, the way we were kept apart really confirmed that we were different. Or, rather, that we should believe we were different. We, according to the layout of our school, needed to be separate. Anyone looking at our school from the outside would see a diverse school—students of multiple different races and ethnicities all together in one building. But once we were inside, our classrooms reinforced the segregation that we had been taught was a thing of the past.

We were tracked.

Tracking is when schools group students together based on their test scores, school performance, and perceived (or supposed) capabilities (some of which were based on stereotypes). A mix of school officials, administrators, and teachers decide which students will be placed in which tracks. There's always an academic college–preparatory track, but not everyone gets the chance to be in that. There's usually a vocational track that prepares students to join the labor force. And there's often a track that's more general. Usually tracking happens in middle school and high school, but it happens in elementary schools too, just on a smaller scale. There, students get placed into leveled reading, math, and spelling groups.

Tracking helps keep schools segregated, and White students are the ones who benefit most from this practice.

Folks who are proponents of tracking will argue that all students, regardless of which track they are placed in, benefit from being among classmates and peers who are at the same academic and social levels as they are. Arguments are made that being in a classroom with students of wide and varied abilities is unfair because students won't receive the more focused academics and attention they deserve. And to an extent, they are

TRACKING

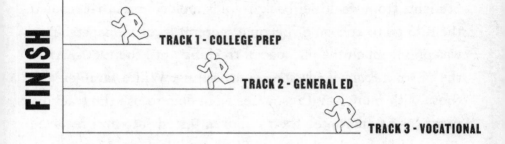

not wrong. Students who are tracked with kids who have similar test scores and schooling skills do well in classrooms where teachers can hold higher expectations and have to differentiate less, and they learn in greater depth. But the reality is not all tracks are created equal and treated equally. The practice of tracking leaves schools greatly divided and segregated within. Walk through most middle schools and high schools and you will probably be able to tell which classes are filled with students who are labeled Team One or "college-bound" or who were tracked into that academic lane. Those classrooms will most likely have more White students; they'll have an abundance of resources (compared to some of the other classes); and you'll see teachers who are genuinely engaged with their students. Many districts across the country, my old one included, have a great racial disparity in their upper-level classes.

Tracking is a normal part of the way schooling is done in this country. It began as a practice early in the 1900s. Poor folks, working-class folks, and immigrants were placed in paths that readied them to become members of the workforce—farmers, plumbers, factory workers, builders, and so forth. Students from wealthier backgrounds took courses that readied them to go to college or become secretaries or managers. This was pretty much the purpose of tracking until the 1960s. After the *Brown v. Board of Education* court ruling, White families and those with money and resources were able to use the tracking practices to guarantee their children tested into and received elite and higher-level classes. Black families, immigrant families, families of the Global Majority, and poor families were purposely left out and left behind and tracked into lower-level classes. This hasn't really changed much over the past decades, other than it might be called something other than tracking depending on where you live.

Tracking sets us up to believe that students who do well on tests are more deserving of time, funding, energy, and resources than students who don't score well.

Technically, tracking can be an illegal practice. Title VI of the Civil Rights Act of 1964 prohibits discrimination in programs that receive federal funding (like public schools). It prohibits discrimination in grouping students based on their abilities (or, tracking). The act states, "No person in the United States shall, on the ground of race, color, or national origin, be excluded from participation in, be denied the benefits of, or

92

be subjected to discrimination under any program or activity receiving Federal financial assistance."

Schools and districts are not allowed to segregate students and assign them to specific schools based on their various social identities.

Schools are not allowed to discriminate and segregate students by creating class assignments based on their various social identities.

Schools are required to ensure that students are not mislabeled and placed in incorrect and inappropriate special-education programs.

Schools are required to ensure that students of the Global Majority, particularly Black and Latine students, are not mislabeled and inappropriately placed into the special-education track.

Schools are required to educate all students equally regardless of what identities they hold and intersections they navigate.

Schools may not use special-education placements to segregate students.

Schools are not allowed to segregate students who are learning English for the first time.

Schools are not supposed to use ability grouping or tracking as a way to segregate students.

Schools are not allowed to . . . they are required to . . . they are not supposed to . . . they may not . . .

But they do.

And tracking and ability grouping persists and persists with

93

voracity in our districts and our schools.

Tracking is prevalent in many, many schools today. It's inescapable. It's sneaky too, because, wherever you end up, whichever track claims you, you are convinced for a little while that that track is where you belong. This happens because you don't get a chance to see or experience what happens beyond your lane. But when you're there, you have a sense that something's not right. You can see the differences when you wander the halls or talk to your friends. You can feel the shifting attitudes of the teachers and administrators—they adore some kids and despise others. You can hear it when the classroom doors are open.

Tracking replicates the unjust and racist hierarchy that exists within our society. It continues to be a tool of suppression and oppression. It guarantees that some people in society will succeed and hold more power and some people will not. Tracking guarantees that we will continue to have folks who are excluded and exploited, and those folks are almost always Indigenous, Black, and Brown People of the Global Majority. Tracking ensures that the unjust and racist hierarchy that we hold as normal is maintained. Tracking feeds the racist system that created it.

LIZ

Liz's Story

By Liz Sohyeon Kleinrock

"Coach, I wanted to let you know that I won't be at practice tomorrow."

"Why not?"

"It's Rosh Hashanah, one of the Jewish High Holy Days."

"What? You don't look Jewish."

What does that mean? Would I look more Jewish if my skin were paler, my hair lighter, and my eyes a different shape? Would I look more Jewish if I weren't Asian? Would I look more Jewish if my face "matched" my name?

"Um, I am."

"Have your parents write me a note, then."

"Yes, Coach."

95

GARY

Stains We Can't Ignore

By Gary R. Gray Jr.

When I was told that Jackie Robinson was the first Black man to play Major League Baseball, I had already fallen in love with Ken Griffey Jr., Derek Jeter, and Joe Carter: the Kid, Captain Clutch, and Mr. 1993 World Series Game 6. I knew little about sliders, extra innings, and pinch hitters. I knew even less about why only 16 percent of the players looked like me, my pops, and my favorite Black superheroes: Blade, Black Panther, and John Henry. I wanted to know more about these Black men, beyond the diamond and stadium fences. Like, whose house did they visit for the cookout? How did they find the perfect barber for a lineup? And which of them had watched my favorite movies, like *Set It Off*, *Boyz N the Hood*, and *Juice*?

I knew baseball as a team sport before I knew soccer and basketball. I was seven years old when Dad bought my first mitt and I started fast-pitch. For us, baseball was not just a game; it was also a family affair. A family whose members all happened to live down the street from one another—Brooks, Downey,

Smith, and Simmonds. All Black families, born and raised in Preston, where everyone was your auntie or uncle, first, second, or third cousin. The rest of the league was all white; no ashy elbows, no backward hats like Griffey, no screaming Black mamas in the bleachers, and no sweet potato pie after the game.

In the 2000s, I watched Vladimir Guerrero, C. C. Sabathia, and Prince Fielder continue to transform the sport that tried its very best—but fell way short—to look like my uncle Hank and uncle Elroy. It was my turn to join the "Big Leagues." I told myself I'd move away from fast-pitch played among family and toward hardball in a neighboring white community. I took my bat and my adult-size glove, which was way too big for any child but had been on sale at Walmart and had a black Ken Griffey Jr. signature on it, all the way to the city. The diamond was cut differently there; the chalk was extra white, the dirt was unusually clean, and the grass was always trimmed so fine.

Smack!

"Run, Wheels, Run!" Dad cheers, bending forward and pumping his left fist. Dad's voice somehow rises over everyone else's.

As I round first base, Coach screams, "Keep going, Keep going!"

From the dugout, teammates repeat, "Get down, get down."

"Yourrrrr're out!" shouts the tucked-in-blue-shirt man, pounding the air in a downward motion.

I stand up. Wipe down my pants and notice red stains on my socks and outside leg.

"Nice shot. You almost had it." I shoot my helmet toward the bench, pivot, and race back to second base for fielding as Austin tosses my enormous glove squarely into my left hand.

A voice rips through my button-up Cardinal jersey and into my chest: "If you had any more dirt on you, you'd be a ni**er."

The only other time I heard that word was on *106 and Park* and *Rap City* when my moms and pops wasn't watching, the mixtape scene was booming, and Jay-Z, Lil Wayne, Nas, and Young Jeezy were making unheard-of amounts of music. Southern rappers such as Nappy Roots, Ludacris, Lil Jon, and Three 6 Mafia started to take over and I taped every hit song on my cassette recorder and listened to it over and over and over again.

Austin and I freeze, our gazes locked, unsure why he said what he said or why it is wrong, but we both know it's wrong and that we have to do something about it.

Option 1: Pray about it, because that's what we do in the Black community.

Option 2: Skip the praying and punch homeboy in the mouth until we draw blood.

Option 3: Live with it, laugh, and shrug it off.

In that moment, I remember wondering how my baseball superheroes prepared for fastballs, curveballs, and change-ups daily. Who washed the stains from the polyester and nylon pinstripes they got from sliding into second base or trying to steal home? What did they do in nail-biting situations, knowing that every choice they made was being watched and had consequences?

"Ma, how you gonna get those stains out?" Mama scrubs those polyesters and nylons with bleach.

Today, as much as I try to separate myself from the stains on my uniform, those marks are not easily removed. That day was frustrating and confusing, but since then, I've decided that I will be the one to determine what those stains represent and how they influence my next at bat.

My stains will serve as a reminder that words matter; they have the capacity to empower and influence others, as well as hurt and confine them. They can have long-lasting and life-altering impacts.

"Did you get it?" I ask Ma as she finishes scrubbing.

"Boy, all that dirt ain't gonna come out, and that dirt ain't gonna determine how you play the game." Ma rinses her hands in the sink to get the excess bleach from under her dirty fingernails.

Thanks, Ma.

You right.

MY HIGH SCH

MY HIGH SCHOOL

Another building named after another White guy.

My high school was named after a Syracuse mayor elected in 1950. He was the city's first Democrat mayor in a quarter of a century. I went to our neighborhood school, the same one my mom did. It was the only high school we ever considered attending. The main entrance to the school is tall and striking in its plainness. It's kind of unwelcoming too. To get inside, students are funneled down a few stairs or a ramp and through the doors. Once inside, the first thing you see is the cafeteria. Its bright overhead fluorescent lights greet you way too early every morning.

Several different middle schools feed into this high school. (It's the same for the other high schools in the district too.) It's more of a campus compared to the other school buildings I was used to. In fact, my old middle school could comfortably fit inside. This high school is not one giant building but three, all connected by bridges and stairways.

First, there's the A Building. It's where most of the academics happen for over thirteen hundred students—science labs, language classes, math, English, and the library. They're all tucked into windowless classrooms. Every corner of this building is a stairwell. The A and B Buildings are connected by two bridges that are all windows, a nice reprieve from the forced fluorescence of the halls and classrooms. The bridges span a little pond and some greenery. They're one of the rare sources of natural light in the school. The B Building is home to the gym, the pool, and most of the arts and vocational classes. Next to it, connected by a short staircase, is the C Building. It's where the auditorium, band, and chorus spaces are. The back entrance leads to the student parking lot. Beyond the parking lot you'll find tennis courts, playing fields, and a sloping hill with a path that leads to the track and football fields.

WHAT I LEARNED DURING MY FRESHMAN YEAR

My freshman locker was in the B Building, and I often had to cross bridges and navigate flights of stairs to be prepared for class. I loved the flow of people on the bridge. Unlike in middle school, I got to see the other students in the hallways, in PE class, in the cafeteria. We weren't as isolated. But we were still segregated. I carried my Team One status with me wherever I went; it never left me.

I unconsciously departed from many of my middle-school friends. We stopped writing notes to each other; we didn't talk on the phone as much; and, while we were friendly, we stopped eating lunch together. We were often in different classes. Our interests changed and we gravitated toward different things and different people. A bigger school with more students from more places offered me new friendships.

I found my people. Or, rather, I found some people who were my people throughout high school. With them, I didn't feel like I had to change myself to fit in. I felt like I got to be more of myself even when I wasn't so sure who I was becoming. I joined the drama club. There, I got to invent and reinvent myself if I wanted to. In my first role, I dressed up like a wooden ventriloquist doll and lay flat on a table for nearly the entire play. I think I had one or two lines, and I loved it. I was a part of something with other people. Drama club was where I could be whoever I wanted to be, and the people around me—they, too, could be whoever they wanted to be. I didn't feel like I had to fit myself into a little box. It was exciting.

I lost myself in middle school and slowly collected myself in ninth grade. Freshman year was the year I started to trust myself. I started learning how to take my internal list of questions and verbalize them so I wasn't holding everything in all the time. I stuck to my beliefs. I asked questions and spoke up. I didn't try to make myself invisible. I formed opinions that were my own, not the ones I thought would please my classmates and peers and teachers. A new school with lots of new people allowed me to start becoming myself.

In middle school, my band director didn't want to teach me how to play the drums. Instead, he pushed piano lessons on me. In contrast, my band director in high school was patient and not afraid to teach a girl how to play the drums. I learned how to drum in high school. I stood in the back of the band room

105

and learned how to play the vibraphone and tune the timpani drums. I learned how to roll on the snare and graze the ride cymbal.

For once, I felt like I had some autonomy in my learning. I had the ability to choose a few of my classes, choose my friends, and choose what my impact could be. Of course, my old Team One badge of privilege and power helped give me some of the confidence I needed. Teachers automatically trusted me. They held high expectations and praised me with number and letter grades that I was proud to take home. The labels I carried told my teachers I was an exceptional kid . . . even though I wasn't any more special than any other kid in that building.

I continued to learn about European and American domination in the world as if it were victorious rather than shameful. I continued to be labeled *gifted* and sat among mostly White students in a class with a teacher who was fast approaching a midlife crisis. We continued to read books by deceased White men.

Freshman year felt like a fresh start even though school was the same as it had always been.

AUGUST

August's Story

By August

In my school there was a policy that we had only three minutes to get from one class to another. There were a lot of people in the hallway and my school was two stories. If you didn't get to class in time, they were supposed to lock the door and send you to the office to call your parents. Me and some of my friends, who were all Black boys, got to class a little late, but we got there at the same time as other students who were white. When we tried to explain why we were late, we were sent to the office, but my teacher accepted the other students into class. I was angry because it felt like he offered them a second chance because he looked like them, and he didn't believe us because my friends and I did not look like him. I didn't get into trouble with my parents, but things like that made it hard to trust white teachers even when they probably thought they were just following the rules. I got suspicious that they were always looking for me to mess up and that

107

when I told them the truth about something, they didn't believe me anyway. I sometimes wondered if telling the truth was worth it if I was always going to have to do extra to explain myself.

WHAT I LEARNED DURING MY SOPHOMORE YEAR

I was a drama kid. I was obsessed with Jonathan Larson's musical *Rent*. All my drama-club friends were. We knew all the lyrics. We sang every part of the musical until our voices became hoarse and we all sounded like Daphne Rubin-Vega. That musical allowed us to explore our identities through song and dance, and we were able to try out being different people. We raised funds, held a garage sale, and sold all of our teenage prized possessions, then we chartered a bus and hightailed it out of our midsize city for a day. We saw *Rent* on Broadway. We wanted to be those actors onstage. Somehow, we all saw ourselves in the cast. Whether it was Mimi's hair or Mark's ability to observe from the sidelines, Collins's love for his friends or Angel's innovations—we saw ourselves in the cast and characters because we desperately wanted to.

Unfortunately, but realistically, there was much more to

school than drama club. I embraced my savior side and joined our school's international relations club. We worked with the Peace Corps Partnership Program to raise funds for volunteers we were connected with. We sold beautiful notecards (designed by students) and T-shirts (made by alumni) and raised thousands of dollars to build latrines and medical centers. I was so proud to be a member of that club. I was driven by wanting to do good; Gandhi's quote "You must be the change you wish to see in the world" propelled me forward. I felt like our club was making a difference. (And maybe we were.) I didn't recognize that my own community could have used that funding to ease the costs of school lunches, school supplies, and winter gear. We never went deeper or tried to understand the decades and centuries of institutional misuse and abuse of power that led to kids needing to hawk notecards at craft fairs to raise money for necessities of life.

***

My AP European History teacher posted our grades on the wall every week. We saw our rankings. We saw who was at the top with the highest grade, and we saw who was at the bottom with the lowest. Once I got to the top, I wanted to stay there. I learned to value competition and did my work for the grade rather than for the love of learning. I learned about English kings, wars, and how to write a document-based essay. I also learned how to strive to be the best, to want to be at the top of the class, to work toward what I believed to be perfection, and to value the progress I was making over the process I was taking.

Whether it was purposeful or not, my teacher forced competition on us. The great tool of shame and fear was used to motivate. I totally fell for it. A lot of my classmates did. Instead of encouraging collaboration and setting us up to learn from our mistakes (individually and collectively), my teacher divided us with the little numbers posted next to our names each week. In an odd and messed-up way, our teacher was preparing us to be in a society where the culture of White domination rules the world.

LORENA

What I Remember (Part Two)

By Lorena Germán

I remember the first day of high school when the ninth-grade class was brought into the auditorium and told that half of us wouldn't make it to graduation. The shock was deep, and the questions lingered. I looked to my left and right and wondered who wouldn't graduate and why. I also committed to making it because my immigrant parents hadn't come all the way here for me to fall to some statistical or mythical monster that makes you fail. The moment is one I've yet to forget, and I'm thirty-six. And all the teachers stood in the back, like guardians of the space, like prison guards blocking our exit. They said nothing. Their silence was loud.

I remember in tenth grade when my PE teacher was looking to argue with me because I had testified before the city's school committee. She must have figured instigating a fight was the excuse she needed to get me suspended. I knew she'd have administrative support, so I didn't let her win. She made sarcastic critiques about my testimony when I asked to use the restroom and when I wanted to take a break if I was talking to a peer. Literally, any chance and she stepped right in. She didn't appreciate what I was saying at these meetings because it revealed that the teachers (in general) were not there for us. How could they not have mentioned that many of our bathroom stalls were missing doors? How could they not have mentioned that sometimes the heaters didn't work and we sat in class with coats, hats, and gloves on (for those who had them), trying to complete classwork? How could they not mention that the only bathroom in the gym area for physically disabled students also had no stall? How could they have missed that if they were indeed "for the children"?

I remember in senior year being questioned by the teacher for standing at my locker between classes. She got close up in my face. She opened her mouth wide. I remember smelling her lunch. She screamed so loud. At that point, though, I wasn't the one. I had developed the rough exterior necessary to deal with these white teachers. I gathered my belongings, slammed the locker, and, with the mature calmness of an experienced racism-resister, told her she would also be in detention, considering she was also not in class. "What are *you* doing in the hallway?" She stood in shock, probably at my self-advocacy more than anything else.

I wish I didn't remember all of this.

I wish there weren't even more memories.

I wish I could forget.

And I think that what I learned is that white supremacy

doesn't just look like white men, real scary-like, in robes, with pitchforks, violently screaming racial slurs at us. It can look like white women who don't care. Who don't listen. Who are there to collect their paychecks and see their "tough love" in our communities as charity. Who want their friends and acquaintances to see their daily drive across town (of course) as their way of doing "something great" for "those kids" and making their country a better place. And white supremacy can be calm, quiet, sitting at a desk, following the rules, saying things beneath its breath, not calling on us, not walking over when we're sick, mocking us, absent forever, laughing with each other in the hallway, and simply being part of a system that is killing us. All while wearing cute sweaters in craftily decorated classrooms.

WHAT I LEARNED ABOUT SUICIDE

Before we even really started our second year of high school, a classmate ended their life. And then, some months later, another classmate did the same.

It was devastating.

We were wearing green because it was St. Patrick's Day. A friend and I were snacking on Cheerios because our teacher didn't mind us eating during lessons. We welcomed the unexpected disruption from one of the school counselors. We didn't know what was happening or why some students, including me, got pulled from class.

We made guesses: Were we going to a secret party? A celebration? Something exciting—I was certain it had to be something exciting. But the counselor gave us no clue about what we were about to walk into.

We buzzed with curiosity, smiling and laughing with each other.

We walked down the stairs, crossed the bridge, went down another flight of stairs, and ended up in the auditorium.

We were thrust into a storm of tears, strewn papers, and crumpled, sad, confused bodies.

A counselor told us of our classmate's death. There was no mention of the word *suicide*.

Our principal, or maybe our school counselors, or someone had decided to corral some students in the auditorium and tell us about our classmate's death. They collected us together and forced anger and grief out of us and then they sent us back to class. I don't know how or why they chose the students they did. While we were in the auditorium, our teachers and other students tried to carry on, but the news got around school, and carrying on and acting like things were normal and okay wasn't possible anymore.

The school totally mishandled it.

I don't know if there was any protocol or policy on how to support a group of teenagers, their teachers, their caregivers, and their community when death by suicide comes to school. It felt like it was being made up as the day went on.

I wish my classmates were still alive today.

I wish things were different.

In October 2021, several institutions that support children and teens (including the American Academy of Pediatrics, the

American Academy of Child and Adolescent Psychiatry, and the Children's Hospital Association) put out a statement declaring that our country was in a state of emergency when it came to the mental health of children and adolescents: "This worsening crisis in child and adolescent mental health is inextricably tied to the stress brought on by COVID-19 and the ongoing struggle for racial justice." Suicide is one of the leading causes of death for young folks ages ten to twenty-four. During the first year of the COVID-19 pandemic, the rate of adolescent deaths by suicide increased. According to the CDC (Centers for Disease Control and Prevention), emergency department visits related to suicide increased by 31 percent for folks between the ages of twelve and seventeen. Social distancing, being disconnected from classmates and peers, teachers, and school communities, lack of mental-health care and support, anxiety over family economic and health problems, and an increase in substance use all likely contributed to the increase in suicidal ideation and suicidality.

We never talked about suicide in school. We never talked about mental health either.

While the rate of suicide attempts has been on the decline for adults, this is not the case for children and adolescents. Suicide is preventable. There are things our schools and institutions can do to better support folks.

We are living in an incredibly divided country. A few adults are loudly advocating for the removal of books that serve as lifelines for so many of us who do not fit neatly into the dominant culture. And some are trying to push SEL (social emotional learning) out of schools for fear students will learn to be compassionate to folks who are different from them. Not only is division a part of the status quo, we are placed into boxes with labels that give some of us power and privilege and deny it to others. We're taught to be binary thinkers and believe that there is only one proper and right way to do something. We're encouraged to be perfect because perfection will prove our worth. The culture of White domination keeps us disconnected from one another and from ourselves. Fear is the driving force, and suicide is often driven by fear. We fear things that remain unspoken and unknown. We fear being different, being unliked, being not good enough, not knowing that we can be connected and that we are more than enough all the time.

Schools can be and should be places where we are connected to others. If we're encouraged to work collaboratively, to learn and engage in discussion with each other, we're connecting. If the focus of schooling becomes less about getting the best grades and more about community, we'll be more connected and accountable to one another.

PATRICK

The Othering

By Patrick Harris

I went to school in Southfield, a predominantly Black working-class suburb right outside of Detroit. Southfield is located north of Eight Mile Road, only fifteen minutes from downtown Detroit. To this day, Detroit is one of the Blackest cities in the United States. Growing up in Detroit and exploring the South during family reunions, I spent my childhood surrounded by Black people. And yes, I knew white people existed—some of them were my teachers—but I never saw white people in big groups except on television or in movies. This was about to change.

In the year 2008, during my freshman year of high school, I was intrigued by Business Professionals of America (BPA). BPA is a national organization that prepares "tomorrow's business leaders today." Students from around the country learn analytical, critical, and creative skills that prepare them not only for careers in business but also for competitions. My best friend,

119

Shaunte, joined the club with me. Our BPA team was small, no more than five students. Our adviser was named Ms. Banks, but we called her Latisha behind her back. She was a professional businesswoman turned teacher in her second career. She was knowledgeable and helpful and pushed us in her own chaotic way. Throughout the year, we met several times to develop our presentations for the competition. I had decided to compete in the Individual Presentation category. My challenge was to give a presentation that planned the next BPA conference.

Preparing for the competition was not just about learning the latest business models. My adviser wanted us to be prepared to compete against white students. This meant extensive conversations on professional business attire, with her commenting that we were representing not just our teams but "our school, our family, our community." We took the bus to Grand Rapids for our competition, and we were held on the bus until we "had it together"—we had to have our professional attire checked by our adviser. It was more than just wearing a tie correctly or ensuring a blazer was the right fit. This was about making sure that Black kids from Detroit could assimilate with white kids from across the state of Michigan. Entering the convention hall turned on my anxiety like a light switch. Knowing that I was different, I constantly checked myself; I walked slower, stepped into the bathroom multiple times to ensure my tie was on correctly, shushed my teammates when they laughed too loudly in the cafeteria. When it was time to compete, I took my laptop into the room, set up the projector, set up the PowerPoint, and asked if the judges were ready. The judges were two white women in their late twenties. They worked in the advertising sector and had volunteered to judge the competition. I started off well, just like I had practiced with my teammates and my adviser at school and in the convention lobby moments before. As I was attempting to tell the judges about our Los Angeles conference, I stuttered. I could not focus on my words because I could see the judges smiling too big, holding back laughter, and snickering together. They bonded with each other until the end of my presentation. "Thank you," I said procedurally; they responded with "Good job," and I walked out feeling defeated. I went to my adviser with wet eyes and told her that I was not good enough to be taken seriously in my first competition. Her first question was "Were they white?" She knew the answer to this. I nodded; she lowered her eyes, and her eyebrows sharpened. She told me that I had done the very best that I could and that she would handle it from there. Without further questions, she went to file a complaint with the conference officials. At the awards ceremony, with no surprise, I learned that I had not placed in the top three and would not be moving on to nationals, despite my business attire, despite the amount of time I spent practicing, despite doing everything right while Black.

I had learned how not to stand out in the company of white people, but this did not create a safety net when the othering came. When the discomfort showed, my toolbox was empty.

The very thing I had been talked to about had happened, and I had not learned how to manage my feelings when I had felt discriminated against. Nor did I know how to advocate for myself. I had no understanding of how the system worked. I just knew things were unfair and I was different.

I grew up in a Black neighborhood and went to a Black school. Having pride in our Blackness was something that I had without question. But when it came to interacting with white people, the emphasis on pride was absent. May Black kids who leave their neighborhoods and see the world never lose themselves by trying to gain the acceptance of others deep in a system that depends on seeing Blackness as inferior. May they try their best in all they do. May they be able to understand when racism stares them in the face and laughs in a whisper, and may they not flinch. Instead, may they lean into their pride and their power that lives inside.

SHEA

The Fat Black Kid Who Flew

By shea wesley martin

I met Vaughn Ambrose before I learned to love jazz more than food, before jazz taught me to love my Blackness more than anyone else ever could. A stocky dark-chocolate tenor saxophonist and music teacher from the backcountry of North Carolina, Mr. Ambrose (or Ambrose, as we called him) blew sounds from his tenor saxophone that commanded respect from everyone—even the kids like me that were always getting into something. The summer I met Ambrose, my mama signed me up for a music camp. The program, designed for rising fourth graders, allowed students to try instruments before instrument selection in the fall. I don't know why my mama signed me up. I loved the drums, but she loved the saxophone, so that's what I would play. On Sundays, she twirled me around our basement to Grover Washington Jr.'s "Mister Magic," but I had no interest in playing the saxophone until Ambrose's horn wailed while the faculty jammed to "Chameleon" at a camp talent show. I was hooked, and it was all Vaughn Ambrose's fault.

My love of the saxophone lasted through "Hot Cross Buns." But my love of music, of being heard in my rawest form, pushed me all of the way to graduation. Ambrose would be my camp teacher for the next two summers and throughout middle school. Interspersing his lessons with stories about gigs, history, and trips to perform and attend concerts. He brought the Yellowjackets, a famous jazz combo, to our school's dingy auditorium, and when one of the kids asked Marcus Baylor if he could play go-go, he did, and that beat made it on their next album. I followed Ambrose to green rooms to meet jazz legends. I borrowed his CDs and begged for hall passes to hear about his latest shows.

In the early 2000s, being a fat Black kid obsessed with jazz made me an alien. That was fitting, though. Jazz took me to another world. In jazz, my mama wasn't sick all the time; she still danced and smiled from hospital beds. In jazz, I wasn't ashamed of my Blackness. Ambrose's classes offered me what other classes didn't—another universe, where Blackness was king; where my story was still being written; where I could wail, blow, and moan and call it creating and dreaming. Like my math homework, jazz was hard, but *it* made space for me. When I was blue, I put on Lee Morgan's "I Remember Clifford" and listened to the ballad Benny Golson wrote for Clifford Brown after his death. On the days I felt my best, I bopped and floated above the clouds in the sounds of Herbie Hancock's synthesizer.

When I moved on to high school, Ambrose came to run the high school band program. By high school, my reputation preceded me. I was the fat Black kid with "so much potential" who "needed to try harder." I slept my way to Bs in honors classes and sketched out songs instead of taking notes in math. *I still can't believe I passed geometry.* While my trajectory seemed ironclad in my "academic" classes, band continued to be a space of liberation, joy, and creativity. Ambrose said that jazz was about loving the music enough to get lost in it long enough to find yourself. So, I got lost and learned to change keys, improvise, and fall in love with my own sound. That's what jazz was—love and change personified. So, when I went to Ambrose in tenth grade and told him I wanted to switch instruments in the school's jazz ensemble, he didn't blink. I had seen a video of Lionel Hampton smiling and playing "Flying Home." I was meant for the vibraphone, I said. I would practice more than I ever did at the saxophone, I promised. He smiled. I never practiced my saxophone. Ambrose relented. The next day, I walked into my counselor's office and told her I wanted to give up my lunch period to join the concert band so I could be the next Lionel Hampton.

"You're already in two other music classes, Martin," she argued. "When will you eat?" she asked.

I smirked and asked her if she had ever heard "Flying Home." I told her it would change her life. The next afternoon, I walked into concert band with extra granola bars in my backpack, picked up my mallets, and prepared to fly to a home where joy, Blackness, and possibility were never-ending.

WHAT I LEARNED ABOUT MILITARY RECRUITMENT

I was set on taking as many science classes as I possibly could. I dreamed of becoming a medical researcher and discovering a cure for cancer. I took chemistry and I took an extra science class my junior year. The Syracuse University Project Advance (SUPA) biology course excited me. It was a real college biology class taught by an actual college professor (well, kind of taught by one). The class was different. We got to learn at our own pace using tapes created for us by the professor we never met. (The tapes were old, and we didn't get all of the outdated jokes and references, but they were also pretty funny.) The class was a mix of juniors and seniors. It wasn't a free elective. Our caregivers had to pay a fee for us to attend the SUPA class, but it was cheaper than taking it at the actual university and we received course credit at the end.

I remember how uninvolved the teacher who ran the class was. It seemed like she was really only there to make sure we had the materials we needed. I think she liked our group. We didn't ask a lot of questions and often worked with headphones on. I liked the unfamiliar autonomy I had in that class. We used microscopes to analyze our blood and spit, made Punnett squares, dissected small creatures, and figured out which of our traits were dominant and which were recessive. My brown eyes are dominant. The fact that I can't roll my tongue into a tube is recessive, a gene I must have gotten from my dad. I learned about the disease that had taken out all of the Dutch elm trees in our city before I was born. And I learned that school didn't have to feel like a grind.

***

And I was in my fifth year of learning Spanish too. I was beyond proud that I sometimes dreamed in my second language. My twin and some of our peers from Señor Ogden's middle-school class continued on beyond the four-year requirement we needed to graduate. We learned how to conjugate, read, and write in Spanish. It was the class where I felt most relaxed and challenged and motivated and excited to learn. We were a small number of students in a corner classroom on the third floor. Our maestra had a German name and a love for Cuba. Señora introduced us to *La Catrina*, a made-for-school telenovela about Jamie González and her summer abroad in Querétaro, México. We loved it. It was the thing that connected us. Our maestra

127

had the highest of expectations for us and didn't let us get away with mediocre accents and negligent translations.

Our maestra didn't teach out of a textbook. She didn't make us copy verb conjugations into our notebooks and try to absorb them through rote memorization. In her classroom, we learned the truth about how the sanctions against Cuba affected the people living there. We learned about socialism without her actually saying *socialism* and how 99 percent of the Cuban population was literate while our own country's rate was about 80 percent. We learned that it was okay to take a day off and watch *Harry y los Hendersons* (again). And we learned that patience is possible in a school setting.

***

I liked being a junior in high school.

I know not everybody did.

I was getting myself ready to grow again, to grow beyond my family and our home, to grow beyond my friends and our city. Junior year, for me, was the calm before the storm of college applications and big decisions. I knew I wanted to go to college. I'd been planning on it for years. I was tracked for it, from being admitted into the gifted and talented program in sixth grade, to being a Team One kid in middle school, to being encouraged to take all the right classes to get a Regents diploma. I was college-bound. My twin and I were the first in our family to set our sights on attending a four-year college. It felt thrilling and powerful and totally daunting.

Our school's one college counselor suggested every time we

met (which wasn't often) that I look at his alma mater. I didn't. I thought I knew exactly what I wanted. While I didn't know which colleges I wanted to apply to, I thought I knew what I wanted in a school: I wanted to go to a small, liberal arts college in New York State. I wanted to stay somewhat close to home and my family. I wanted a school with a strong science department and a theater program. I wanted to be challenged and make new friends.

I didn't know how I was going to afford college. I didn't know how to apply for financial aid. I didn't even know what FAFSA was an acronym for. (It stands for Free Application for Federal Student Aid.) I knew I needed scholarships to be able to afford a private four-year college. I didn't know that student loans were way easier to procure than scholarships and that they weren't actually free money. I didn't know that student loans would leave me in debt for decades. Our college counselor checked in to see how our applications were going and helped us get fee waivers because applying to college cost money. He listened to us when we told him where we were hoping to go and was happy for us when acceptance letters came through. He was one person trying to support a whole lot of college-bound teens. And there were a lot of kids in my grade who probably never even stepped into his office, who never even made it onto his list of college hopefuls because we were all tracked to that very moment. Our schooling years readied us (or not) for this final push into whatever our distinctive personalized destinies would be.

Before I seriously started considering which colleges to apply to, I began getting calls from recruiters. People called our house asking to talk with me or my twin about joining the military. The Marines called. The army called. The navy called. The air force called. The Coast Guard probably called too. It seemed every branch of the military thought I could be a good fit. They called during the week and in the evening, usually after dinner when I was sitting on the couch doing my homework and impatiently waiting for my favorite prime-time television shows to start.

Recruiters from the different branches of the military reached out to try and pique our interest and find out if we were ready and willing to belong. They wanted us to know that they wanted us and hoped we wanted them back. They eagerly invited us to join the military family, a long-standing, uniformed (and well-funded) tradition in our country.

Somehow my name made it onto a list of potential military personnel.

***

My school gave me up because they kind of had to.

The military has been recruiting young adults for decades and even centuries. Recruiters tend to spend more time trying to enroll folks who are members of communities that are historically excluded and marginalized. Their targets are often students in low-income and predominantly Black and Brown communities. In 2017, over half the enlisted active-duty labor

130

force were thirty years old or younger. Most active-duty members of the military had high-school diplomas, but less than 10 percent of active-duty members had associate's degrees, and only about 13 percent had bachelor's degrees. The majority of the officers in the different branches of the military had bachelor's degrees, and many had more advanced degrees.

MILITARY RECRUITMENT

ACTIVE DUTY MEMBERS OF THE MILITARY WITH ASSOCIATE'S DEGREES

ACTIVE DUTY MEMBERS OF THE MILITARY WITH BACHELOR'S DEGREES

Why does the military recruit kids while they're still in high school? Younger folks who join the military tend to stay in the service for longer as they work to build a career within their branch.

Our military is voluntary. There is no longer a required military draft (mandatory enrollment). That ended in 1973. But individuals who are born male, who are U.S. citizens or immigrants living in the country, are still required to register with the Selective Service within thirty days of their eighteenth birthday. If you are an immigrant, you have to register within thirty days of your arrival in the country. The Selective Service is a government agency that maintains the database of those who could be drafted into the military if needed. And although there is currently no required draft, Congress can reinstate a draft at any time.

In 1982 Congress passed a law that gave the Department of Defense

131

permission to collect information (names, addresses, phone numbers, age, and level of education) about high-school students who are seventeen years of age or older and students who are in eleventh grade or higher. Because the military is a volunteer service, the army, the Marines, the navy, the air force, and the Coast Guard work in communities to get young folks to join up.

In 2001, as part of the No Child Left Behind Act, Congress ruled that all schools that received federal funding from the Elementary and Secondary Education Act (ESEA) had to provide military recruiters the same access to their students that colleges, universities, and employers had. This included directory information and in-person recruiting. The U.S. military spends billions of dollars on attraction, recruitment, and enlistment efforts each year. Most colleges, universities, and employers do not have a comparable recruiting budget.

Joining the military can be a way for young adults to gain access to resources they don't have in their own communities, particularly if they are living in poverty, living in neighborhoods that have been historically excluded and exploited, or are immigrants or the children of immigrants. The different branches in the military offer food, housing, community, and skill-building. Some offer recruits the chance to travel the country and the world, and many offer support with obtaining a college degree.

My school gave me up to the recruiters. A lot of schools in the United States give up their students to military recruiters. They do it because they're required to.

***

While schools are required to share your information with military recruiters, they must also offer you a way out of being recruited. Sometimes this comes in a form that you can sign at the beginning of the school year. Other times they'll put information on how to opt out in a letter or the school handbook. There's no one consistent and obvious way. Some schools give you the chance to opt out only once—when you enroll in or transfer to a high school. Once you opt out, your school can no longer share your information with military recruiters, and the recruiters will stop calling, emailing, visiting, and so forth. Your high school can still share your information with college, university, and job recruiters, and you can still interact with recruiters, depending on the role they play in your school.

The military also gathers information about you from a database called Joint Advertising, Market Research and Studies (JAMRS). JAMRS is an official program of the Department of Defense. One of its goals is to "explore the perceptions, beliefs, and attitudes of American youth as they relate to joining the Military." It maintains a registry of millions of teenagers and young adults in the United States. Information like your name, address, birthday, standardized test scores, race, ethnicity, and so much more is contained in JAMRS. You can also opt out of JAMRS sharing your information with military recruiters. The New York Civil Liberties Union has a form that you can complete and send to JAMRS on their website. You may also contact your local chapter of the American Civil Liberties Union for help on opting out of JAMRS sharing your information.

I didn't know I could opt out of the calls. I don't remember anyone giving me that option. Because of the laws that are part of the No Child Left Behind Act of 2001, your school is required to give information about you to the military whether you asked it to do so or not. Students should be able to opt in if they want to be recruited; your information shouldn't be something that can be coerced out of your school or bought from a database. You should be able to have that say.

***

The phone calls sounded convincing. The recruiters were kind and excited and enthusiastic. They were confident and knowledgeable. They were authoritative and held ranks that sounded and seemed and were important. The recruiters told me my college could be paid for and my experiences would grow. They were persistent. Even when I told them I wasn't interested, they still called. I was not interested. I was not interested in joining, but they kept calling throughout my junior year and into my last year of high school. My White classmates did not receive as many calls. Many of them did not receive any calls. Other Black and Brown classmates of mine continued to get calls just like me. No colleges or universities tried to get me to enroll as aggressively as the military tried to get me to enlist.

I learned that my life was more superfluous than some others'. There are risks when joining the military. I am the daughter of a Vietnam veteran, and, like so many, I watched the first bombs and cruise missiles hit their targets during the first hours of the Persian Gulf War on television. I learned that my good grades and my enthusiasm about attending college wasn't going to be enough; school still cost a lot of money and the recruiters reminded me of that. I learned that even when I said, "I'm not interested," it didn't matter. I still got a call . . . and another . . . and another. I learned that my school could sell me

134

out without me even knowing it. I learned that the military and the government and the education system—which (I thought) was supposed to be watching out for my best interests—colluded in hopes of getting kids like me (poor and Black/Brown and academically motivated) to head out into the world and defend the United States even though the country was rarely willing to defend me and people like me.

DAVID

David's Letter

By David Ryan Barcega Castro-Harris

Hey, 15-year-old David,

It's future you checking in.

I could tell you things like:

- Straight hair? Bad idea, unless Taboo from Black Eyed Peas is what you're going for.
- Snowboarding? Only if you want to break your (other) arm.
- Deodorant is an everyday necessity, not just when you play sports.

You'll learn those lessons on your own and probably be better for it, but on a more serious note, I really wish you knew that:

- You're not less of a person because you're depressed. It's okay to ask for help when you feel low.

136

- Social media is a necessary evil, but stay as personally detached as you can.

But those are future problems—let's talk about now! I'm really proud of you! You've got so many interests and are currently juggling so many activities, and that's so cool. By next year, you'll be captain of both the varsity basketball and volleyball teams, percussion section leader in a concert band, and lead singer in another band, and you'll still maintain straight As. Around this time, you'll start hearing things from your peers and teachers like:

- "Of course you're good at sports, you're Black."
- "Of course you have rhythm, must be those African roots."
- "Of course you can sing, all Filipinos sing."
- "Of course you're good at math, you're Asian."

You might be thinking to yourself, but those are *good* stereotypes, right? At least they're not using racial slurs or bad stereotypes, labeling me a "thug" or a "dog-eater." True, but these stereotypes let us know that people only see us for our identity and what we can do for them—it doesn't give us a sense of belonging. These stereotypes also dismiss the hard work it took to build these skills and earn these positions. Sometimes hearing these things makes us feel like we

137

don't deserve what we've earned. DON'T let people steal your shine!

- You have some natural physical gifts (yes, the 31-year-old out-of-shape us can still dunk), but you don't become an All-League performer in two sports by just jumping high. You put in more physical and mental training than most of your teammates and opponents.
- Becoming a section leader is as much about skill (which you have) as it is about dedication to the team and your ability to communicate well with your section mates.
- You're not the most naturally talented singer—this wasn't in our gene pool (Your dad is alright, but your Filipino mother is tone-deaf)—but you get better with hours of practice.
- You're smart and good at memorizing and following directions, but you get good grades in math specifically because your elementary teacher mom taught you "touchpoints" for counting at an arguably too early age **and** your former college math professor dad has devotedly helped you through long multiplication and division problems from fourth and fifth grade on.

I wish I could say it gets better, but these kinds of microaggressions aren't going to stop after high school. As you see more of the world through college, travels, the workplace, and the business world, you'll see more of the ugliness. Our world is changing, and people like us are both creating and getting more opportunities to do some really awesome things. And sometimes, folx who aren't used to people like us succeeding in new places are going to be upset and say and do some ugly things. While that's their problem, not yours, and while it doesn't stop hurting, it hurts less as we build community that affirms us for who we are, beyond and including our racial identity.

Keep shining, kid,
—Future You

TORREY

Torrey's Story

By Torrey Maldonado

Me and my boy Russell are in our school stairwell with our classmates heading upstairs to our next class.

"Hold up." He taps me.

"W'sup? Class is about to start."

"Chill. Just. *Chill.*"

I wait, watching kids leave the stairwell until we're alone.

"I need you." He's serious. "C'mon." He turns and hops down the stairs two steps at a time.

"Where you goi—?"

He pauses and whisper-growls: "Shh. Just follow."

Huh? We have class. But at the same time, I can't let him go whereevs solo. He's my boy. Plus, he said "I need you" so serious.

I fly down the flight. As I get close, he exits the stairwell, and I shadow him into a new stairwell. This'd be a fun game of tag except not now since class starts soon and we racing away to where I've never been.

Soon, little things say we're behind the lunchroom. Before he speeds up again, I grab his forearm. "Stop. Why we here? And just us?"

His free hand shoves open an exit door, and we see outside. I'm bugging about right now. Plus no alarms rang? "How come these doors—?"

"Let's be out," he says.

"Russ, if we cut—"

"You know you want to. Why stay here? In wack classes? With messed-up teachers?" He snarls, "This racist school."

Now I'm bugging because he right.

I want to leave.

Our classes are wack.

Our teachers are messed up.

Outside feels less messed up than this school that's just like middle and elementary schools. I don't want to skip but, at the same time, I *want* to skip, y'feel me?

Right now, I hear my mom in my head: *School's your shot.* I'm Ma's youngest. It's junior year and I could be the first in our family to go to college. I want to follow Russ so bad, but I walk away. "Nah."

He yanks the door shut, whisper-hissing at me. "Be a nerd."

I shrug. "A'ight."

He huffs, "Fine," and catches up to me. "C'mon. You know history'll be trash. Mr. R. is mad racist. Why he says

141

'¿Comprende?' when he corrects Latino students? He doesn't say that to white kids or anybody else. And his Black jokes?"

He's right. Mr. R. is racist.

Russ rolls his eyes. "And English? Ms. L. ignores us participating and only picks white kids."

True.

He stops walking. "Nah, I'm not going back to classes. After them, it's Mrs. Z. Why you make me take her elective? Now *you* can't stand her after she last dissed you."

He's right again. Mrs. Z. offered an elective called the History of Resistance, which sounded lit. Then one week of her discussing white people suffering and fighting back turned into weeks of her focusing only on white people. So the other day, I raised my hand. "It's great to learn white history. Will we learn how other people suffered and reacted too? Like, this country was taken from the Native Americans. Or we could learn how Black people were made slaves in the Americas. And how my people reacted."

Mrs. Z. smiled how fake people do when they scheme to hurt or hustle you—all teeth with sneaky eyes that don't smile. "Well," she said, "if you have lesson ideas, maybe become a teacher someday."

A few minutes later as our class discussed something else, this white girl—Kyra—raised her hand. "When you compare the Jewish Holocaust to the enslavement of Blacks, about as many Blacks were killed as Jews. Maybe more. We studied the

142

Holocaust. Maybe let's study Black enslavement and how they suffered and reacted."

"Excellent idea." Mrs. Z. clapped. "We should."

Russ whispered, "Kyra stole your idea. Coming from you, it's bad. Coming from Kyra, it's excellent."

Right now, Russ snaps me out of that memory. "So?"

"Yeah, school's dead," I say. "But I can't cut." I don't say I can't cut for the same reason I had almost perfect attendance in my racist middle school: Because Ma says school is my shot out of our projects.

"Ugh." He huffs. "Now watch how racist Mr. R.'ll flex because we late."

Russ is right again. When we open the door, Mr. R. stops teaching and focuses the whole class on me and Russ. "No pass?"

We shake our heads.

"So it's okay to arrive this late?"

I try apologizing. "Sorry, Mr. R., we—"

Mr. R. wags a finger. "I didn't say speak. I'm marking you both as cutting because—"

Russ interrupts, pointing at a white girl—Karen—who does whatever she wants here and gets babied. "Mr. R., she comes later than this at least twice a week. You never stop class to embarrass her." He points at a white boy—Jerry—who is basically a male Karen and gets babied too. "And Jerry strolls in late. You give him breaks. You give"—now Russ points at other

143

white kids—"her, her, him, him—them all special treatment. But you clown and punish us because we're Black and Latino."

Every white kid here knows he's right but puts on an innocent face. I wish one would defend us.

Mr. R. tells Russ, "It's not about race. Take responsibility. Don't deflect. You're marked as cutting unless you serve detention."

We sit.

"See?" Russ whispers to me. "How'd I say he'd be?"

I nod and look at the white kids, wondering how school would be if we were treated like them.

WHAT I LEARNED DURING MY SENIOR YEAR

Our senior prom's theme was "Save the Best for Last" and we partied like it was 1999 (because it was!). We'd made it. We navigated block scheduling, bad poetry, confusing equations, our first weapons search, science experiments gone wrong, gang fights, required volleyball units in PE, bomb threats, and so many other things. We'd somehow gotten through to the end. And, somehow, we did it together. We didn't all like one another. We didn't all know one another. But we had been through a lot. And we were a community.

My senior year was when I learned how to use my voice. I once stood up in the middle of my physics class, frustrated that my teacher constantly called on the boys and allowed them to speak out and over the four females in the class, and I said some kind of chastising statement that silenced my classmates and the teacher. I was frustrated that year. I was tired of being in classroom spaces where, if you were male and White, you could do whatever you wanted. I learned that outspoken, overly confident, assured White boys could make racist jokes, and the teachers did nothing. I learned that it was okay for those same White boys to gaslight me and try to make me small. Senior year was the year I learned that, apparently, it wasn't strange at all to have a White male teacher mansplain how to alleviate period cramps. I learned that Advanced Placement English meant reading more "classic" books by deceased White men was normal and so was watching *Blazing Saddles*, a movie from 1974 filled with racist stereotypes and unfunny jokes. (I opted out of class that day.) My senior year was the year I learned I needed a break from White boys and White men, so when I was admitted to a small, all-female college in the Finger Lakes region of New York State, I eagerly accepted.

WHAT I LEARNED ABOUT WEAPONS SEARCHES

There was one Thursday during my senior year that was really different from any other Thursday. It was unexpected.

We entered the school building the same way we did all other days. But once we were inside, we were ushered to the enclosed bridges that connected one building to another.

We couldn't go to the cafeteria.

We couldn't go to our lockers.

We couldn't go to our classes.

We couldn't leave the building.

Some of our teachers and administrators waited for us behind tables, small metal detectors gripped tightly in their hands.

We were asked to wait.

We were asked to surrender our backpacks, bags, purses, anything we'd brought into school.

We were asked to take off our jackets and coats.

Everything we brought with us into the school building was touched and moved and checked.

We were told if we didn't comply, we'd face disciplinary action.

Most complied. A few did not. One walked away.

Some wanted to call their caregivers but were told the school pay phone was broken that day. It wasn't.

We had to wait.

We couldn't go to our lockers.

We couldn't go to our classes.

We had to wait for two hours.

We waited for the teachers to find weapons. In the end, they confiscated less than two dozen perceived weapons—knives, scissors, and other sharp objects—from over thirteen hundred of us.

Six students were given five-day suspensions because of the search.

We were upset and filled with rage.

We didn't know it as we left our homes early that Thursday morning, but we were about to take part in our district's first whole-school weapons search.

School officials needed to have "reasonable suspicion" to search our personal items. The superintendent justified the violation of trust in a letter to our caregivers. He wrote, "While our schools are safe, many of the communities they are located in have experienced violence in the past months." He then went on to explain that he needed to take immediate action to keep students in my high school safe. He shared that the search was conducted because "a considerable number of reports came to us from parents, students, police, and community members that weapons may be brought into the school." He ended his letter by offering this advice to our caregivers: "I encourage you to speak with your son or daughter about the importance of continuing to comply with school district policies and rules related to safety and security."

However, a district official told the local newspaper that there was no specific threat to our school on that Thursday. The school-wide weapons search didn't need to happen that day. The superintendent said the search, a two-hour disruption, had occurred in "a timely manner" even though we missed two classes. The search was to "to send a clear message to students." We lost trust in our teachers, administrators, and district leaders. The superintendent wanted us to know the district would not "tolerate any weapons or potentially dangerous objects" at our school. But the message that came across to us was that the superintendent and school administrators did not know us or care about us, and they wielded so much power they could disrupt our entire day whenever they wished.

While district officials claimed the search was necessary and justified, others (lawyers and professors of law) questioned the constitutionality of widespread blanket searches. The superintendent used his power and approved the search our principal requested even though it was not based on any clear evidence.

The laws and policies around such sweeping whole-school searches of students' personal property are broad and vague. The Fourth Amendment of the Constitution does apply to students in schools, but not completely. Basically, it protects people from unwarranted searches (and seizures) by the government in their homes. It's not exactly the same at school. In the 1985 case *New Jersey v. T.L.O.*, the Supreme Court concluded that while the Fourth Amendment does apply to students in public schools, officials do not need to have probable cause or warrants to conduct searches. The laws and policies around school searches are confusing and vary from state to state and even from city to city. You will need to check with your local jurisdiction to get the specifics on what is and isn't legal in your school district.

Schools need to have what's called *reasonable suspicion* in order to conduct a search. And, once again, the term is loosely defined. Here are some examples of what's reasonable suspicion in schools and what isn't:

The smell of marijuana in the hall does not provide reasonable suspicion to search *all* students in the school.

Students reporting that another student has a weapon does provide reasonable suspicion to conduct a search of the student and the student's locker.

A group of students together with their hands in their pockets or holding money or anything else does not provide reasonable suspicion to search anyone.

Reasonable suspicion does not require school officials to have actual clear, objective evidence (like our principal and superintendent at the time). The Supreme Court wrote that reasonable suspicion is "a common sense conclusion about human behavior upon which practical people . . . are entitled to rely." If reasonable suspicion relies on a "common sense conclusion" about the behavior of people, then what impact does implicit bias have on determining whether there actually is reasonable suspicion for school officials to conduct searches of students and their things?

School administrators, faculty, staff, and district officials are more likely to target Black and Brown students when using reasonable suspicion. A study to determine whether Black students were disciplined and punished more than White students found that teachers attributed the behavior of White students to their having an off day while the same behavior from their Black students was seen as a disturbance that warranted punishment. Another study from the Department of Education found that schools with populations of more than 50 percent students of the Global Majority were four times more likely to conduct suspicion-less searches using drug-sniffing dogs. Reasonable suspicion to justify and conduct searches is often clouded by the implicit racial bias that the decision-makers have.

***

Whether the search is being conducted by a school official or a police officer, you have the right to refuse the search. You do not have to consent to be searched. If your principal, the school resource officer, or a teacher ask you if they can search your locker or your backpack, you can refuse. However, schools may

SCHOOLS WITH >50% STUDENTS OF THE GLOBAL MAJORITY WERE 4X MORE LIKELY TO CONDUCT SUSPICION-LESS SEARCHES USING DRUG-SNIFFING DOGS

discipline you for not consenting and some schools have policies that require students to consent. Check to see what your school's (and district's) rules and policies are, and if they are not clear and easily found, ask for them to be made accessible to all students and the community.

Schools may search students if there is reasonable suspicion.

Schools can conduct random searches of students in school.

Schools may not target individual students in random searches.

Schools can conduct blanket searches of all students.

Schools may search your locker without your consent if the locker is considered school property. (Your school must tell you that your locker is school property and not personal property. This policy can often be found in the student handbook. If you cannot find clear information on this, ask for it!)

Schools may use drug-sniffing dogs in searches, and they must have reasonable suspicion to search your personal belongings.

Schools may have metal-detector searches, but the searches

of students must be random.

Schools may not force students to take drug tests. (The exception to this is if you are in an extracurricular activity where random drug searches are conducted.)

Schools may not use evidence found in an illegal search against you in court.

You have the right to refuse to be searched by school officials and police officers in your school.

WHAT I LEARNED ABOUT STUDENTS' RIGHTS

In 1969, in *Tinker v. Des Moines*, the Supreme Court ruled that students do not "shed their constitutional rights to freedom of speech or expression at the schoolhouse gate." Justice Abe Fortas, in the majority opinion, wrote, "In our system, state-operated schools may not be enclaves of totalitarianism. School officials do not possess absolute authority over their students. Students . . . are possessed of fundamental rights which the State must respect, just as they themselves must respect their obligations to the State. In our system, students may not be regarded as closed-circuit recipients of only that which the State chooses to communicate. They may not be confined to the expression of those sentiments that are officially approved. In the absence of a specific showing of constitutionally valid reasons to regulate their speech, students are entitled to freedom of expression of their views." You have rights. You have rights in school.

Your school is responsible for keeping you safe while you are there.

You have the right to express your opinions. You may speak up and out. You may even hand out flyers, information, and petitions. However, you may not disrupt school or violate school policies.

You have the right to share your opinions on social media, and your school may not punish you for content you share when you're not in school.

You have more rights in regard to protesting and sharing your opinions outside school spaces than inside.

You have the right not to salute the flag and not to participate in the Pledge of Allegiance or the national anthem without repercussions.

You have the right to dress in clothes that are consistent with your gender identity and your gender expression. Schools cannot require you to wear clothes based on your assigned or perceived sex. They cannot create a dress code based on gendered stereotypes.

You have the right to not be treated differently based on your sex or gender.

You have the right to not be targeted based on your gender identity or gender expression, race or ethnicity, religious beliefs, who you love, abilities and disabilities, and so on.

You have the right to receive a free public education.

You have the right to go to school if you are undocumented, and you do not have to prove your immigration status. Your school cannot require you or your family to prove your immigration status.

You have the right to attend school whether you have a home address or not. It is illegal for public schools to turn you away.

You have the right to receive language instruction regardless of what your home language is.

You have the right to extracurriculars, and your school cannot deny these to you because of your disabilities.

You have the right to equal access to all aspects of your education, and your school is required to make accommodations for you.

Your school is required to address and respond to harassment, discrimination, and bullying.

You have the right to privacy and no one (including school and district administrators, faculty, and staff) should "out" you to your family, classmates, anyone.

You have the right to join or form a Rainbow Club, a Gay-Straight Alliance, or any LGBTQIA+-related club if there are other clubs that aren't related to classes taught at your school.

You have the right to be kept protected and safe; your school cannot ignore bullying, harassment, and so forth because of who you are and the identities you hold.

You have the right to keep your transgender status private. Your school cannot disclose this information without your consent. You are protected by the federal privacy law.

You have the right to join in classes, extracurriculars, and school events without fear of punishment for being a pregnant or parenting student.

You have the right to not be punished or excluded for having an abortion.

You have the right to keep your private medical information private; it cannot be shared with anyone without your consent.

You have the right to attend doctor appointments and to take time off for giving birth and healing from childbirth in a judgment-free environment. Your school must provide accommodations for you if you are pregnant or have a medical condition that is temporary.

You have rights. You have rights in school.

MY
COLL

WHAT I LEARNED DURING MY FIRST YEAR OF COLLEGE

College was a culture shock.

I attended my first-choice school. It was a small women's liberal arts college not far from home. I was tired of being talked over and ignored, especially in my science classes. I didn't want to have to compete for airtime anymore. I wanted to focus on learning. I wanted to be in a small, nurturing environment where I could get to know my classmates and my instructors. I received a decent scholarship in my financial aid package. And, unlike so many other colleges, this school actually reduced tuition to a realistic amount. It was an easy yes for me.

The college was in a very small rural town. On warm days you could smell the newly sprayed fertilizer from the nearby farms. The center of town contained a small inn, an opera house that was once a jail and a library, and a general store that also served as the local pizzeria.

The campus was small, and the college was situated across the street from one of the Finger Lakes. I could see the lake from the small window of my fourth-floor room and once I took an exam on the boat dock rather than in a classroom. The school prided itself on its honor code. We all signed it during our first days on campus. Rarely did folks lock their doors. People left books and work piled in corners of the library and computer labs knowing they would be waiting for them untouched or un-tampered with when they returned.

I didn't have a great experience with my freshman-year roommate. In fact, it was awful, but that's a story for another day.

I chose the college because I wanted to attend a small college. I chose it because I needed a break from overly confident White boys. I thought that a small women's college was my best option. A liberal arts education appealed to me because I wanted the ability to explore other disciplines. I met young women from other places, mostly in New York State and New England. Nearly everyone I met was White. We were from different socioeconomic backgrounds, had different beliefs and politics, and we all existed in the bubble the college built around us with its culture and way too many traditions (that took up multiple pages in the student handbook) and ghost stories. One of those stories was about the founder of the college, his mistress, and his wife. We were told that if you were walking across the little bridge that connects one side of the campus to another and the light went out, you shouldn't look back because the founder's wife could be following you with a knife, thinking you were the mistress. Despite the ghost stories, our world was small and White and sugarcoated.

We were told if the lake froze over in the wintertime (which it rarely did), it was because the freshman class were all virgins. That day would be marked by the cancellation of classes. There was a congratulatory song that was sung often, at birthdays, celebrations, and so forth. Everyone was supposed to know it. The lyrics were in our student handbook. We even had a traditional afternoon tea on Wednesdays. We took a break from seminar and met up in the art-exhibit room for tea and cookies. There were also multiple traditions for each class to perform every year, from organizing a hayride to singing songs and playing basketball to kissing the feet of a statue of Minerva. Unfortunately, I was not a fan of participating in traditions. They were never mandatory, but participation was expected.

It was rumored that there was a local chapter of the Ku Klux Klan nearby. I hated walking alone on campus at night. I never went to town on my own. I never felt comfortable at the small college I'd put all of my hopes into, and I quickly fell out of love with the school and its isolated community and transferred out of there.

OZY

Ozy's Story

By Ozy Aloziem

When I first tried to write about the impact race and racism had on my educational experience, I found so many different moments that they filled an eighteen-page single-spaced document. When I read through what I had written, I realized that there were no stories surrounding the joy being a Black student has brought me.

This isn't to say that those moments don't exist—they do, though there might not be many. But I have witnessed that throughout my entire education, whenever race was brought into the classroom, it was done in a way that problematized my experience as a racialized student. That is, it was done in a way that focused on how terrible it was to be a Black student in the U.S. school system instead of on how bad U.S. school systems were to Black students.

I believe that there is a way to talk about racism in our school systems without problematizing what it means to be racialized.

Black, Indigenous, and other students of color aren't the problem. The problem is the ways in which school systems in the United States treat Black, Indigenous, and other students of color.

If I had to sum up everything the past two decades of schooling have taught me, it is that I have to do my best to hold on to my wholeness. Racism, especially racism in educational spaces, has taught me that this world will do its best to reduce you to pieces.

I felt this first in elementary school. As the child of two Nigerian immigrants, I sort of knew what it meant to be African American and African, but I didn't understand what it really meant to be Black or even racially marked. I remember winning a spelling competition in the first grade, and my friend, another Black girl, getting upset and calling me *darkness*. I remember being so confused that someone who looked so much like me could be so hurtful in such a specific way. The first time you see something about yourself as a flaw changes how you see yourself forever.

I felt this in middle school. I attended a very diverse Catholic school with limited resources. Our school was a part of the Archdiocese of Omaha, and once a year, all the Catholic-middle-school students in the archdiocese attended a church service together. On the short bus ride to the church, we would make jokes to prepare ourselves for what we were about to experience. Most of the schools that attended this yearly meeting were predominantly white. When our bus pulled up and we poured out, the students would turn and stare at us. The othering that occurred was palpable, and my classmates and I knew it, even if we didn't have the language to name it. We attempted to find humor in our discomfort. "Caucasian overload," we'd whisper to one another as we filed down the church aisles. On the bus ride back to our school, we would discuss what we had just experienced without actually getting to the heart of it. Our teachers said nothing.

I felt this even more in high school. I attended a Catholic all-girls high school that prided itself on creating empowered young women. One of the most expensive high schools in Omaha, it had a prestigious reputation. It was also predominantly white. Out of almost six hundred girls, there were twenty-one Black students. I knew all of them by name and knew each of their respective stories. All our teachers and administrators were white, and they didn't seem to understand the impact this had on the school and its students. I was often the only Black student in advanced classes. I was never exposed to a curriculum that validated my experiences or knowledge. The race-evasive approach the administrators utilized allowed them to ignore all the ways in which my white peers were prioritized. My Blackness was noticed only when it benefited my white classmates or teachers. When my school wanted to highlight its diversity, it called on me. When my high school decided to host a So Hip-Hop It Hurts–themed homecoming, as the resident expert in

Blackness, I was called upon to braid hair and offer outfit suggestions. My success at the school hinged on me appealing to the interests of my white classmates and teachers. I often felt that the only reason I was there was to be of service to the white people; they assumed they had the right to demand it.

While I often felt picked apart because of my race throughout my education, I was able to have my race centered in important ways both inside and outside of those various classrooms. These spaces made me feel full and whole and taught me that I ultimately had control over my wholeness, that I could find and choose what felt good and mine.

In middle school I joined my school's speech team and quickly fell in love with poetry. I discovered the work of Maya Angelou and used her words as an anchor throughout the rest of my middle-school and high-school experiences. I participated in my high school's speech team, and that space was where I first discovered that a classroom could actually feel safe for a person who looked like me. I found classmates whom I could be myself with, a teacher who saw me and wanted to support me, and a place to freely express myself through poetry and dramatic interpretations of my favorite texts. And though I still hated my high school and tried with all my being to leave, that team was one thing that kept me.

In high school I was also a part of the diversity club. We came together because we felt a distance between us and our white peers. Our meetings were about issues we faced, and we problem-solved how to best navigate those situations. I found sisterhood and joy within that space. We made a home for ourselves where we could exist specifically as students of color in a school dominated by whiteness that refused to acknowledge its racism.

I also participated in an academic program designed to funnel students of color into college. During the summer, I took classes at a university with other students of color from various high schools in Omaha. Outside of the academic classes, we attended sessions that focused on helping us develop ourselves as scholars. I was able to explore a variety of professional fields while being introduced to research. I participated in that program for four years and learned so much. It allowed me to be mentored by professionals who looked like me, and it gave me the opportunity to form relationships with people who understood my lived experience. I felt empowered as a Black student and received significant identity development that I hadn't previously had.

My junior year of high school, I went on a trip sponsored by a local church, a three-week road trip with a group of sixty students I had never met to visit thirteen historically Black colleges and universities. During that trip, on a rainy day in Alabama, I ran through a muddy field in a torrential downpour with a group of kids who had become like family to me, and I felt so free and alive, like I could be anyone and anything I wanted to be. As we collapsed, panting, on the ground, I looked up at the sky and felt connected and infinite and powerful. I was so moved, I started crying through my laughter. During that trip, I realized that life is about more than how others see you. It's about doing things you enjoy simply because you enjoy them.

I will be honest: There were times during my schooling journey when I felt less than whole, less than willing, less than able. I think I lost my way there for a bit, couldn't see past the fog of racism and whiteness. I felt too picked apart and discarded. I forgot why I was there and why me being there mattered. It's easy to feel angry at all the things that have tried to take away my wholeness, my shine. I choose to also remember all the necessary things that had to happen for me to have made it here. All the wonderful ways in which I was encouraged to be the Black female scholar I am. Remembering has been a healing process. While I know the hurt education has caused me because of racism, I also know the joy education has brought to my life and why that's worth pursuing. It is that reminder that keeps me here. I realize that my wholeness cannot be dependent on someone else's ignorance or even systematic oppression. I am more than the ways in which I have or will continue to suffer. How I show up during the mess is my testimony. I can feel the ways in which I heal around the hurt and the softness that emerges as a result of that. I choose to lean into that softness, into that grace.

The trick isn't to brace yourself; it isn't to be constantly on the defensive, constantly looking for the next thing that will hurt you. Instead, it is to turn inward and outward. In toward yourself, to create and find narratives that haven't been shaped by racism, and outward to the people who choose to see you and love you for who you really are. We are more than the ugly ways we are often treated. We are so much more expansive than that.

WHAT I LEARNED ABOUT MALCOLM X AND THELMA & LOUISE

We were given the choice between reading *The Autobiography of Malcolm X: As Told to Alex Haley* and watching the movie *Thelma & Louise*.

The second-semester course was winding down and so was our drawing of conclusions about failure and success in America. We read some books. We watched some movies. I really cannot remember much about the class. It wasn't very remarkable. My professor was a middle-aged White woman whose specialty was English and film studies. I can't remember much about my classmates. They weren't very memorable.

I do remember that we spent a lot of time discussing Mark Twain's book *Pudd'nhead Wilson*. A *lot*. The book was first published in 1894. You might have had to read that book or another by Mark Twain for a class. Mark Twain and his books are a part of what's considered the American literary canon. The canon is a group of books that are considered classic, influential, and *very* important; they are approved, recognized, and often the default standard books read in schools. Sometimes the authors are revered, and their books are deemed to be the most worthy books, the ones that should be read by all. As Wesley Morris said in his *New York Times Magazine* article "Who Gets to Decide What Belongs in the 'Canon'?," "Typically, the people drawing up our cultural canons have been an elite group of scholars and critics" and are White cisgender men. Books by folks who identify as women, Black and Brown folks of the Global Majority, members of the LGBTQIA+ community, and anyone who does not fit into the small box of the dominant culture have traditionally been left out of the discussions and decisions on what should be considered canonical. The American literary canon is a social construct. And, no surprise, most of the authors in the American literary canon are dead, White, cisgender men.

If you've never read *Pudd'nhead Wilson*, I can quickly sum it up for you: It's about two boys who were switched in infancy. One of them was born a light (White-passing) enslaved boy and the other was the White plantation owner's son. The mother of the enslaved boy swapped the babies after birth in hopes of giving her child a life of freedom that he wouldn't have otherwise. The enslaved woman's baby, originally named Chambers, grew up to be a privileged, selfish socialite. The plantation owner's son, originally named Tom, grew up enslaved. There's a lawyer called Pudd'nhead Wilson who collects fingerprints. Wilson serves as the lawyer at a trial, and thanks to his fingerprint collection, the baby swap is revealed. The real Tom returns to being a White man and becomes the heir to his family's fortune, but because he was raised as an enslaved person, he finds that he no longer fits in anywhere, especially in the dominant society. The real Chambers loses his privileges as a White man and returns to being an enslaved person. He is soon sold to pay off the debts of his master. Pudd'nhead Wilson becomes the mayor of the town, but he is not able to enjoy his success because no one in the town really likes him.

I didn't like the book. There are people who do; I am not one of them. That book was not the one we should have read to understand the way racism and socially created concepts like assimilation and enslavement and passing affected people's lives. We could have read *The Autobiography of an Ex–Colored Man* by James Weldon Johnson, or Nella Larsen's *Passing*, or *anything* by Toni Morrison. What failure is and what success is wasn't clearly defined. We worked off the professor's opinion on what failure and success could be in the country, and that was greatly defined by the parameters of the dominant culture. We did not reach a collective consensus. Nor did we create a definition that existed outside the status quo's definitions of failures and successes. The course was really (without it being said) an exploration of the culture of Whiteness (as many college courses so often are). We could have spent our time exploring themes of justice and community. We did not. We could have had discussions about how failure and success are social constructs and then worked to redefine what they mean in a more socially conscious way. We did not. We could have talked about the continued and persistent theme throughout history of social constructs of perceived superiority and the ways in which we have been divided for centuries. We did not. We could have read Frederick Douglass or Zora Neale Hurston. We did not. We could have read texts by just about *any* author of the Global Majority. We did not. What we did do was watch the block-buster movie *Thelma & Louise*. We did that instead of reading and discussing *The Autobiography of Malcolm X*.

Thelma & Louise was one of those movies that was always on television on Sunday afternoons in the latter 1990s. It was released in 1991 and was a hit. It was about two White, cisgender female friends, played by the actresses Geena Davis and Susan Sarandon. (Both actresses were nominated for Academy Awards that year.) Some people criticized the movie, claiming it was anti-men because, unlike many movies, especially ones before the release of *Thelma & Louise*, it centered on the relationship between two women. At the time, the movie was radical.

Louise is a bored waitress. Thelma is a housewife married to a controlling, officious carpet salesman. The friends set out to take a break from their "ordinary" lives. On their way to a cabin in the mountains, they stop to get a drink at a bar, and Thelma is assaulted by a man. He tries to rape her, but Louise stops him, threatens to shoot him, then does shoot him after he insults her. From there, the movie turns into a story of two fugitives on the run to México. They meet up with a hot, young thief. He steals their money, so the friends rob a convenience store.

They continue fleeing to México, in the process locking a police officer in his car's trunk and making a trucker's tanker explode. When the police catch up with the friends at the Grand Canyon, Thelma and Louise make the decision to "keep going," and the movie comes to a close with the two friends choosing to end their lives by accelerating toward the canyon.

The movie was a feminist anthem—or, rather, a White feminist anthem. *Thelma & Louise* was totally revolutionary in the movie industry at the time. For once, women were in the lead. They were making choices and decisions that affected their own lives and many others, and they were in charge of their sexuality and their narratives. The majority of the other top-grossing movies of 1991 had cisgender-male leads. *Thelma & Louise* was a reframing of the way things had always been done in movies. It kind of made sense for us to watch it during a seminar at an all-women's college. Our professors wanted to instill strength and empowerment in us. They wanted us to be good feminists and resist the patriarchy. We were *Women* with a capital *W* and our bond of friendship and womanhood could confidently carry us into the world and beyond those college classroom walls. The movie showed us how to react to and resist the male-dominated society. It showed us we had to always stick with our female friends and that we belonged to an unbreakable sisterhood.

Thelma & Louise was not the story to replace Malcolm X's autobiography. It told us about who could be left out of stories without any thought. There was no representation of Black

174

people, Indigenous people, or People of the Global Majority in the movie or in our Failure and Success in America course. The films we watched were all mainstream movies, ones that many of my classmates and I had already seen. All of the stories we read and watched reminded me that the only stories that apparently mattered were the ones by and about folks in the dominant culture.

We watched *Thelma & Louise* instead of reading *The Autobiography of Malcolm X*! We swapped a book about a very real, transformative, thoughtful, and honest Black leader for a popular movie. This was instigated by our professor. My classmates voted to watch a movie many of us had already seen instead of reading a 527-page book about a Black man who had been demonized throughout history. The choice was the easy, obvious one. A group of young, mostly White women chose comfort.

We really could have read the book. We had multiple classes left in the semester, probably enough to read the book and discuss the themes of failure and success in America. But we did not.

The movie *Malcolm X,* directed by Spike Lee, was released in 1992. It starred Denzel Washington as Malcolm X and Angela Bassett as Betty Shabazz. The movie was a fairly accurate representation of Malcolm X's life. Dr. Betty Shabazz (Malcolm X's wife) consulted on the film. However, we were not given the option of watching the movie. If we were choosing movies over books, we could have watched *Malcolm X* instead of reading the book. We did not. We were assured, as a group of young women on the verge of independence who were about to usher ourselves into a world that existed beyond our caregivers and childhood bedrooms, that the fictitious stories of White women were more important that the real-life stories of Black men, their families, and their communities.

Honestly, I chose that class because none of the other freshman seminars seemed interesting. I was curious about the theme of failure and success in America. By then, the second semester of my freshman year, I was figuring things out and had realized I didn't want to major in biology. Working in a science lab did not bring me the same joy that reading, thinking about, discussing, and writing about literature brought me. I decided to major in English literature with hopes of becoming an English and language arts teacher. When I saw *The Autobiography of Malcolm X* on the course syllabus, I was excited. I didn't know much about him. We'd never learned about him in school.

My professor asked us to purchase the 1992 edition of the book for $14.95. (About three hours' worth of work in my minimum-wage work-study job.) I bought my copy new from the college bookstore. The back room of the store was set up like a warehouse, with white metal shelves stacked with books requested by professors. We had to buy multiple books for the course and I'm sure I spent well over fifty dollars on books for Failure and Success in America. For most of the semester, *The Autobiography of Malcolm X* sat on my bookshelf with other books for other classes. Some of them I read and some of them, like the autobiography, remained untouched.

No one told me that books were going to be such a big expense. I didn't know. But each class has required readings for the syllabus, and sometimes they're very specific editions of books that libraries have limited quantities of. Some books you can rent, especially the more expensive math, science, and language books, but most of the books for my English classes, I had to purchase. I had an on-campus work-study job in the college's theater, building sets and putting information in the box-office database. I made minimum wage for a small number of hours each week. My work-study job was how I paid for books, supplies, and anything else I needed.

Malcolm X spent time with Alex Haley (who was a journalist then) between the years of 1963 and 1965 working on the book. It was published the same year Malcolm X was assassinated. *The Autobiography of Malcolm X: As Told to Alex Haley* is a story of growth and transformation. Malcolm X shared the story of his life, from his youngest days with his siblings, mother, and father, to his father's murder, to his mother's hospitalization, to his time working on trains, living in Roxbury, and hustling. He shared the story of his time of incarceration, his Muslim faith, and his awakening into the great, powerful Black leader he was until his death. In the autobiography, Malcolm X wrote about the time his teacher told him he should be a carpenter rather than hold on to his dream of being a lawyer. We learn that he fell in love with a White woman who betrayed him and his friend Shorty, which resulted in Malcolm's and Shorty's imprisonment. (Malcolm X was sentenced to eight to ten years in prison and was imprisoned for six and a half years.) We learn that, while incarcerated, he read, studied, and copied all of the words in the dictionary to improve his penmanship and gain knowledge.

Malcolm X shared his observations and insight with the readers and remained true to himself. He showed us that humans have the capacity to learn and grow and unlearn and grow and learn and grow again. He showed us the power of words and truth-telling.

I finally read the book the summer after freshman year. I read all 527 pages of the autobiography in two days. I couldn't put it down. I neglected my job, kept my head down, and read. That summer, I worked at a dorm at a local university. There, I sat at the front desk and helped students. My mom drove me to work every morning at five thirty, and at the end of my shift, I either walked the three miles home or I took the bus. Each day was long and, for the most part, pretty sedentary. I read a lot of books that summer. A *lot*. (Working the front desk of a dorm in the summer is pleasantly uneventful.) The only book I remember, though, is *The Autobiography of Malcolm X*.

It was unlike so many of the other books I'd read in my college and high-school classes. It's nonfiction. It told the truth. It's a Black man's story written by a Black man. It's a book about the impact of racism and how it tore the Little family apart and put the middle child of ten into prison for too long. It's a book about the prison system. It's a story about the work of faith and religion and about Islam. *The Autobiography of Malcolm X* jolted me awake, and for once, I felt like I had the language to understand the world around me a little more clearly. It was the language I had been seeking and craving . . . and . . . I was mad.

I was furious!

I was angry that we'd watched *Thelma & Louise* instead of reading Malcolm X's life story. They're not comparable, not in any way. We could have devoted time to discussing the book and diving deep into the theme of failure and success in America. We could have practiced using a critical lens to gain a deeper understanding of the way racism affects us all, of the criminal justice system, of the education system . . . we could have done *so* much with the book. Instead, my professor allowed a movie about two fictitious White women to be a substitute for a book about a very real Black man and his experiences in our country. We spent so much time discussing *Pudd'nhead Wilson* by Mark Twain, fiction written over a hundred years ago, that no time was left to explore a much more recent and relevant person.

In that class I learned that we were supposed to care only about the failure and, even more, the success of White folks. This was emphasized by the books we read and the movies we watched. I learned that the lives of Black people were not supposed to matter as much as the lives of White folks, whether they were fictional characters or very real individuals who walked the earth. This was emphasized by the stories and authors that were left off the syllabus or abandoned at the end of the semester. I didn't actually learn anything about failure or success.

OZY

Ozy's Letter

By Ozy Aloziem

Dear Sister,

I think a lot of people enter college thinking that this will be the place they find themselves, but oftentimes you first lose yourself before that happens. That's what happened to me.

I attend a particularly small institution, which means that you're not really allowed any type of obscurity. And since I'm only one of very few women of color, I've always had this nagging feeling that I have to be extra careful because people will always be aware of me. So I hid things because I felt like I was the only one that felt a certain way or did these certain things. There are certain parts of myself that I was so ashamed about and that list just grew and grew until my life bloomed into this one big source of shame.

But when you hide parts of yourself, you are telling yourself that you are not worthy, not worthy of love, not worthy of acceptance. And eventually this message is so ingrained in your head that you believe it with every ounce of your being. You hate who you are and your body becomes this place you no longer wish to inhabit. Don't get me wrong, when you ask people what they think of me, they typically say headstrong, which I am and always have been, just not about the things that really matter, like myself.

A close friend of mine, perhaps the best friend I've ever had, once gave me some advice that at the time seemed really simple and even silly, but now makes so much sense. He told me to just be me because I was the best at being me and he loved me best for that. Here is someone who knew my most private secrets and thoughts telling me that it was okay, being me and my mess of eccentricities was okay, even beautiful, and he didn't love me in spite of that but because of that.

My point is, I've spent so much time living so carefully, because I've been afraid of disclosing too much or sharing anything at all, because I thought it would make people so put off by me. I have made a lot of mistakes in my life and there are many things I wish I hadn't done or said, but I can't change any of that. I can only rectify or make amends with what I can and change the person that I've become. I've slowly begun doing that, addressing things I ran away from, taking control of my vices, really being me and expressing my thoughts and feelings. This process is a long one and it is never-ending, but I'm learning to be relentless. I'm learning to be unrestrained in my vulnerability. I'm trying to go back to feeling things with every atom in my body, loving so deeply it hurts. I'm tired of looking at the totality of my life, I want to get stuck in the details of it all again. So here's to that.

We are only as strong as the things we let destroy us.

With all my love,
Your sister

In college, I participated in a support group for women students of color called Women's Journey. It was an incredible network of sisters who empowered, encouraged, and embraced one another. Every group meeting began with us sharing a meal together and ended with us all sharing prayers and praise. During the prayers, we talked about the things we were struggling with and asked the group for support. During the praise part, we talked about the accomplishments we were proud of and wanted to share with the group. There was always crying. At my white high school, I never allowed myself the kind of public breakdown I thought only white girls were afforded. Instead, I often buried my hurt deep within myself. So coming into this space was absolutely healing for me. That group was the first place I felt it was okay to publicly cry in, even if it was still within a private space.

Toward the end of each year, we were all invited to write a letter to a sister, real or imagined, about whatever we wanted to impart. At the last meeting of the year, we'd each receive copies of a book of our collected writings, printed and bound, and be invited to read what we'd written. The letters captured what we'd experienced, what we'd shared with one another, and our hopes and ambitions. We were invited to give copies of the book to the "sisters" in our lives. The central message of the book was that as women of color, we never had to journey alone. I've kept a copy of each of the books we created during my four years and have gifted copies to many young women.

WHAT I LEARNED DURING MY LAST YEAR OF COLLEGE

One of the persistent themes throughout my school years was my trying to go undetected and unnoticed during various times in my journey. This was especially true for middle school and during parts of my college experience. Sometimes I tried to remain undetected because I hadn't finished the assigned reading for class. Other times I hoped to passively blend in while I was figuring out the complexities, beauty, and strengths of my own identity. And sometimes it was just easier to try to blend in, relying on the falsehood that I could be just like my White counterparts.

But there were some places where it just wasn't possible for me to not be my full, complete, whole self, especially in college. And, even though I transferred to a bigger college in a small city, I was still, too often, othered. My classmates knew

183

I wasn't like them. I looked different, and my reference points were unfamiliar to them. Theirs were unfamiliar to me too. So many times I heard stereotypes projected into the room as if they were facts. Micro- and macroaggressions sliced through the classroom, opening fresh wounds on the few of us who dared to exist in the predominantly White space. Too much time and energy was given to their actions and, especially, to the mistruths and falsehoods they spilled onto the floor. Those moments forced me to speak on behalf of anyone who shared *any* identities with me—Black folks, biracial folks, Black biracial folks, folks who grew up in a single-parent home, kids of immigrants, people who lived in cities, folks who got weighed at the WIC clinic and shopped for groceries with food stamps, first-generation college kids, and so many other parts of me.

I turned into the self-appointed representative or spokesperson for myself and so many others with shared, historically excluded identities.

This happened in an education foundations course.

This happened in multiple English literature courses.

This happened in a writing class.

This happened in a sociology course I took when I studied abroad.

This happened in a religion and society class.

This happened in my work-study jobs.

This happened daily and weekly and multiple times in a single day.

It almost always started with another student saying, in an

assured, unperturbed voice, something like "In my opinion," or "I'm going to play devil's advocate here," or "Well, I think . . ." (with the *think* drawn out and ending on a higher note). These phrases were followed with one-sided opinions based on stereotypes and littered with microaggressions. This was the normal-speak. It was a normal we were all enveloped in. Other classmates nodded their heads willingly (or maybe unwillingly) and were often drawn to the charisma of the (usually) young, White, cisgender, heteronormative student who spoke with such unwarranted and assured certainty. They spoke with more authority than our professors. Which is probably why the professors rarely (if ever) called them out on their misinformation, bias, and racism. Instead, they left it out in the middle of the room for anyone to pick up as truth or rebut. But if you refuted and spoke truth, you did it at your own risk.

In my default-spokesperson role, I took that risk.

Always, it started with my face growing hot and filling with fire. My body would teem with frenetic energy and propel me forward in my seat, bringing me closer to the center of the room. Thumping and beating, my heart caught the rhythm of the other students in the room who weren't ready to speak truth into the space but needed and wanted it to be said. And then my mouth opened and projected an interruption into the room. Sometimes I knew what was going to fly out, hit the walls, and fall down in the middle of the circle of our desks. Other times, I was not prepared for my words. Regardless, my body, my heart, my brain, and my mouth formed statements of facts that contradicted the overly confident White speaker. It was my truth and the truth of people like me, our experiences that are constantly left out, misinterpreted, ignored, or falsified over and over again.

I spoke.

I disagreed.

I put myself in the line of mistruth, disgust, ignorance, and I didn't like it.

It was uncomfortable.

It was scary.

It was . . . it was unfair.

The professors, the ones with the most power in those college classrooms, should never have opened up the space for such harm. They could have protected me. They should have protected *us*, those who were being spoken ill of, who were being misrepresented because of perceived stereotypes and lack of true knowledge. They could have easily interrupted when nonsense and hurt came out of the mouths of classmates who took up too much space (physically and emotionally). They should never have allowed the damage to be served up to us as if it were something we should just take quietly and with deference.

Our professors should have . . .

They could have done so many things.

But they never did. Even when they did speak up, they didn't say much.

They placated.

They pacified.

They silenced.

They laughed it off.

They wrapped things up.

They redirected and misdirected.

They placed the destruction they'd incited into our hands, asking us to disappear it between the pages of our assigned readings and notebooks, hoping we would forget about it but never let it go.

***

The class was small. It was in a thin, rectangular corner room. The tiny desks (the kind that swung up and over the attached seats) were lined up against the walls and we were forced to look into the faces of the people who sat across from us. Like in all my other classes, the seats were filled with mostly White people. I was one of a few, if not the only, Black or Brown person there. I preferred to sit closer to the door and underneath a window. My friend and housemate sat next to me, to my left. Sometimes our shoulders touched. Sometimes we shifted in our seats at the same time.

Directly across from us sat a White guy with floppy blond hair and a crooked smile. He wore an ostentatious, brightly polished watch on his left wrist. He sat with his legs splayed out in front of him or sometimes spread out wide, and he took up as much of the physical space around him as possible. He sometimes leaned forward, grabbed the little desk attached to his seat, and tilted the whole contraption forward, coming close to falling and moving farther into the center of the classroom.

187

He was the devil's advocate.

He shared his opinion like it was gospel.

He listened for his own voice in any conversation.

He liked when others agreed with him.

He took it personally when others disputed his claims.

I didn't know him. I didn't like him. I didn't think much of him until his insufferable words sliced into my train of thought. He had no regard for people who held identities unlike his own.

He wasn't easy to ignore. He took up a lot of space. Within his arguments (of which he made many), he blamed people. He blamed single mothers. He blamed Black people. He blamed Muslim people. But he never blamed the institutions. He never blamed the systems that oppressed. He never addressed the laws and policies and traditions and culture that forced injustice on us.

And, a lot of us in that room, did the same—we blamed people over systems. Even when we were studying the history of society through different faiths with a critical lens, it was easier to blame people than whole foundational systems and institutions. We put individuals and groups of people at fault for oppressive systems rather than owning up to the reality that there are rules and structures that have been at play to cause division and harm for centuries.

***

Throughout my four years in college, my classmates and I did the work of studying people and the ways their individual selves were exceptional and important. In my educational psychology class, I studied Lev Vygotsky and Howard Gardner and their observations and theories that help us understand young learners better. In my class on the history of modern art, I studied Hilla and Bernd Becher and their extraordinary way of looking at mundane, everyday buildings. I studied Judy Chicago and Cindy Sherman and was awed by their commentary on the role of the female in society. All of my required English literature courses celebrated the works of dead, (usually) White, (usually) European men. I read Bram Stoker, Thomas Jefferson, Homer, Walt Whitman, Dante, Chaucer, Tom Wolfe, William Shakespeare, and so many others. Rarely were books by female authors assigned, and when they were, the authors were almost always also dead, White, and European. We didn't read authors of the Global Majority. We didn't study artists of the Global Majority. They were just completely left off the syllabus.

Everything in every syllabus was so White because my professors were White . . . and most of the students in the college were White . . . and the college administrators were mostly White . . . and the board members were White . . . and the big-money donors were White . . . and because the academic setting I was in maintained the rules of Whiteness as the default, and nobody questioned why.

I thought it was what college was supposed to be like. What I experienced was reinforced by the TV shows I watched and articles I read in popular magazines. I didn't know anything else. And, anytime I questioned the why, I was made to feel and believe I was being too combative or ignorant, a time waster and a disruption to the learning process.

Question the books and the assigned readings on the syllabus—you'll be made to feel small and unintelligent because you're just a student and your professor is an expert in whatever particular field you're studying. They probably have published articles in academic journals to prove their worth. You'll be encouraged to not question the assigned readings again.

Question why nearly all the professors are White—you'll get some answer about how there aren't enough Black people and Indigenous people and folks of the Global Majority with the appropriate degrees. And if you bring up how Black people and Indigenous people and folks of the Global Majority have been purposely excluded from higher education, you'll once again be labeled as a disruption and your question will go unanswered.

Question why there are still way more White students attending your college—you'll probably hear about the diversity and inclusion initiatives of the school. You might even be asked to be on a committee or let your photograph be taken for marketing purposes.

Question why most of the administrators are White—you'll be told the university does an extensive and thorough search for the best candidates for the positions and the (usually White) people who are in those roles were really and truly the best people to fill those various positions. They have all the proper credentials, experience, and references.

Question why the people on the board and the big donors of the college are nearly all White—you'll be told that doesn't matter. The folks on the board had some DEI training a couple of years ago and are donating their time and expertise to ensure the school is headed in a positive, sustainable, competitive direction. You might even hear something like "Anyone can donate to the school" or "No donation is too small." And you won't be given a response that actually addresses your question.

Question why your college (and so much of academia in general) does so much to maintain the status quo of Whiteness and adheres to the characteristics of the culture of White domination—you will be made to feel like you are more than a disruption. You might possibly be made to feel like you don't belong and that your questioning is out of line. You might even be told that you are being racist by calling out racism. (You're not.) You will be dismissed—whether with a flick of the wrist, a dead-on stare, a back turned to you, or a quick phrase like "I think we're done here" or "I can't believe you're bringing this up now."

In my schooling situations, I wasn't taught to be critically conscious. I wasn't taught about oppressive systems, and I definitely wasn't taught that those systems can be dismantled. I wasn't taught to think and act in a more community-minded and liberatory way. I was encouraged (along with all my classmates) to faithfully accept the information that was presented to me from anyone with power and authority as the only truth. I was encouraged to be passive, not to see color, and to be binary in my thinking. And when we just go with it, we're rewarded for our inaction.

Well, some folks are rewarded. Folks who fit into the dominant culture of our society are given opportunities by way of laws and policies and rules that keep them in the position of having more power and more resources. And folks who are historically excluded and marginalized aren't really a part of the reward system. Perhaps a few are so there is some kind of proof that the system isn't totally rigged against us.

But it really is. And it's unfair and unjust.

We know this because the number of Black men who are incarcerated is disproportionate to the number of White men.

We know this because the number of Indigenous and Black people living in poverty is disproportionately higher than the number of White folks living in poverty. In 2020, the median household income for Americans was about $67,500. The median income for White households in the United States was just under $75,000. For Latine households, the median income dipped to about $55,000, and for Black households and American Indian and Alaska Native households, it was about $45,800. And the median income for Indigenous households on a reservation was about $29,000. There's a big and purposeful difference in the amount of wealth and resources people have in our country!

If we are taught at all about the huge discrepancies and injustices in our humanity, we are often told that it is the fault of the people (whether they are individuals or groups). Stereotypes

HOUSEHOLD INCOME

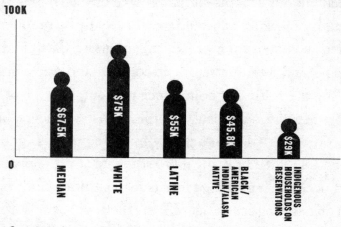

100K

$67.5K — MEDIAN
$75K — WHITE
$55K — LATINE
$45.8K — BLACK/ AMERICAN INDIAN/ALASKA NATIVE
$29K — INDIGENOUS HOUSEHOLDS ON RESERVATIONS

0

become fact and our brains are saturated with falsities. We're taught that Black people and African Americans are poor because they're lazy and prefer to live off government assistance rather than get a job. We're taught that there's an educational achievement gap between Native American students and White students because Native Americans don't have the aptitude for learning. We're taught that Latine folks are all immigrants and refuse to learn English. We're taught that all Asian people and people of Asian descent are quiet and studious and compliant. And none of this is true. They are all stereotypes. They are mistruths.

Institutions collude to keep the stereotypes alive. They work to keep the old status quo that is the culture of White dominance as part of our systems because if things change, power shifts.

The work of racism is very much steeped in power and the

maintenance of that power. Working to keep things "racially balanced" in our schools so that People of the Global Majority, particularly Black folks, would never actually be in the majority anywhere was about power. Not hiring more Black and Brown professors and administrators at colleges and universities and upholding the culture of dominance is about power. Not including more authors, scientists, creators, artists, dancers, builders, and so on of the Global Majority in the course assignments is about power. Not admitting more students of the Global Majority and not offering college fees (such as tuition and room and board) on a sliding scale that reflects the gap that exists between different racial and ethnic groups in our country is about power.

It is the misuse and abuse of power by these institutions that we need to blame, not individuals and groups of people.

I learned a lot of things in college. Some of them were really interesting and great. I learned how to stand taller in my ballet class. I learned how to paint little details on a theater set so the flat wall looked like it had the texture of wood grain. I learned how to make beautiful designs with just a ruler and a pencil. I learned how to write for joy and not just for school. I learned how to live on my own (well, with friends) and to say no and make time for myself. I also learned that people like me, Black biracial, first-generation college kids who grew up poor, weren't supposed to be in colleges like the ones I went to . . . unless they were willing to assimilate into the dominant culture. I learned that it was supposedly okay to leave out the majority of the world population in any thought process, in writing, in discussions, in everyday life. I learned that when I chose to do things differently, to speak up, to write truth that was my own, and to push back against the sugarcoated whitewashed history, I was quickly dealt a hand of naysaying lectures thrown at me by those with the power and those who wanted that power. And those lectures weren't inspiring; they were demeaning and left me feeling less than and second-guessing what I thought was my purpose in the world and . . . it was not okay.

GAYATRI

Notes on Schooling

By Gayatri Sethi

Beloved younger self,

Schooling is alluring.

You will grow up to be a hypereducated person with multiple degrees from world-renowned institutions. You will be viewed as the quintessential girl child from the Global South whom the world declared needed schooling for saving. It will be a widely held belief rooted in saviorism that your life chances and success depend largely on you being schooled. You will believe them. You will be enamored of all the alluring promises of futures possible for you through schooling.

Schooling is a sort of drowning.

You will take to schooling the way that marine mammals frolicking in the Indian Ocean take to the sea. You won't learn to swim well but you will dive deep in school for much of your life. You will dive so deep that you will accumulate many degrees and academic honors gained rarely by people who share identities with you. From the expansive schooling of your life, you will experience a sort of drowning. You will swim through textbooks. You will memorize lessons. You will spend countless hours at school's shores immersed in homework even when not at school. You will deposit the deep-knowledge-diving treasures all over the pages of endless test booklets and examinations. You will be rewarded and disciplined with grades and assessments. You will succumb to these markers of your worth. Your sense of self will rest precariously on doing well in school. You will be called studious and be bullied for it. You might even believe that schooling is all there is to living. You'll become so immersed in schooling that you'll grow up to be an educator. You'll figure out how to drown in schooling cycles all your life.

Schooling is a trap.

The not-so-hidden curriculum teaches you the Western European–centric version of yourself. You learn about world wars. You learn about Europe's heroes. All men. All white. You learn that Africans and Asians needed to be civilized. You learn that British benefactors brought schools to these lands for our own betterment. You learn to read Shakespeare and admire all things European. You even learn to speak French better than you speak Punjabi. You do not learn your own stories through the lenses of the people you share identities with. The hidden curriculum teaches you to perform a certain version of acceptability, respectability, and worth. You learn to look down on your own heritage and cultures. You speak and behave like a brown-skinned Westerner. You devalue your own roots and reject them. You are highly educated but do not realize you are

197

extremely misinformed. You believe you are bettering yourself. You believe you are better. You become elitist, and this is by schooling's design. You become trapped in internalized oppressive ways of being in the world.

One day in graduate school, you will discover the writings of Paulo Freire.

Education functions as an instrument that can bring about either conformity or freedom.

Without freedom, these words are a key that will unlock the trapdoor that leads to drowning in schooling. Your consciousness and, eventually, your school-life choices will begin to shift.

Schooling is . . .

Schooling is a vast ocean of oppression.

Schooling is an entrapment in colonialism.

Schooling is designed by colonizers to oppress while fronting as freedom.

Schooling, for you, has been largely about conformity and not freedom.

Is schooling the same as learning? No.

Is schooling my entire purpose in life? No.

Did schooling prepare me for living? No.

Did learning serve me well? Yes.

Is striving for learning a valuable way of life? Yes.

Is unlearning freeing? Yes.

Unlearning is freeing.

When you gradually tell yourself the truths about how schooling fails its promises, you divest yourself from institutionalized ways of learning. You read widely. You educate freely.

You dive into wells of wisdom and release yourself from the bondage of academic titles and rituals. You become mindful as you relearn the cultural ways of humility, seva, and botho. You refuse to become a colonized oppressor repeating cycles of harm. You begin to unlearn, learn, and relearn new ways of being. This journey is often treacherous but very worthwhile. You might fall into traps and almost drown in oceans of uncertainty, but keep swimming. Keep striving to get free.

As you enrich your mind, keep your heart intact. Protect your soul.

Be well on this learning journey,

Gayatri

DULCE-MARIE

The Story of Doña Ana, Doña Dulce María, and Dulce-Marie

By Dulce–Marie Flecha

Before her hands began to shake, Abuela wrote poems for the New York Yankees. When they came up to bat, she'd open one of her little black dollar-store notebooks and recite her poetry like a man of God. Not like the priests she gave her hand to after mass. Like a subway preacher pushing their way onto the D train in the middle of an afternoon rush hour. Like her words muscled hanging curveballs into the right field bleachers.

I want to tell you the story of how I inherited Dulce María García de Polanco's power. I tried. I've written the first paragraph of this essay over and over and over, hunched in coffee shops, crammed between bodies on the uptown 4 train, sprawled on the summer grass while listening to the shrieks of sirens and car alarms drift into the park from Fordham Road. I have that paragraph littered all over my sala, scribbled, carefully retraced, scribbled again, maybe with a new line break, maybe with "seats" instead of "bleachers."

Before her hands began to shake, Abuela wrote poems for the New York Yankees.

Over and over and over.

I want to tell you the story of how I earned my Abuela's name. But it would be fiction. I have no memory of that. The memory carved into my bones is of Abuela, the brown of her hands contrasting sharply against the sterile white hospital gown, fingers wrapped awkwardly around a pen. The doctors had asked her to write her name. It took her two minutes. She forgot the accent on the í. The doctors took notes. When one—Dr. Chen?—asked Abuela how she was feeling, Abuela dropped the pen onto her knees.

"Yo era Dulce, pero ahora soy amarga."

"Oh," Dr. Chen sighed before turning to the team of white men behind her. "She was sweet, but now she is bitter."

"Ahora ella es Dulce," and Abuela waved a shaking hand at me. "Ella es Dulce y soy amarga. Yo escribía poesía . . ."

She wrote poems.

I sat on the windowsill near an older woman in pearls, a hospital ID clipped to her suit's collar, who asked me if Abuela had any hobbies.

"I didn't know she had stopped writing," I told her, my eyes wet, my arms limp.

***

The earliest memory I have of my schooling is of my Grandma, Ana Flecha, teaching me how to correctly coil my fingers into a fist.

"And if anybody hits you," Grandma said, fluorescent light bouncing off the beige walls of her bedroom, "you hit them back. Don't ask no questions. Hit them back."

Dulce María was Dominican, with a voice she crafted to match her aesthetic. Ana Flecha is Puerto Rican. Both moved through the Caribbean, through borders, through languages, through cultures, through the Bronx. But they had very different philosophies on movement. Abuela's movement inspired poetry. Grandma's movement resisted. Ana Flecha, a veteran of U.S. colonialism, a dropout of the educational system that banned Spanish and the Puerto Rican flag, made sure I knew how to do physically what a colonizer's education forced her to do linguistically and spiritually. Grandma taught me how to defy, how and when to hit.

I've moved around education to some less conventional spaces. I've spent five of my eight years in education working at alternative settings, a homeless shelter and an Office of Refugee Resettlement–certified foster care agency for unaccompanied and separated migrant children. I kept Abuela and Grandma in my pocket while I moved.

***

I can't think of an eloquent way to tell you that I care about pedagogy for highly mobile students more than I care about any other singular aspect of education. It's my soul work and my academic interest, both halves of my professional self. Mobility lives at the intersection of inequities: racism, ableism, homophobia, racism. I want to study them all. I currently work at a school that dedicates itself to serving children in foster care, and I love it. I read research, books, blog posts about homelessness, foster care, migration, usually while shoving an ice cream sandwich in my mouth and calling it lunch. I engage in webinars from the National Child Traumatic Stress Network and scribble notes in my planner on the implications of trauma and autonomy of narrative. I am Dulce María's tocaya and granddaughter; a child of language and poetry. But I am also Ana's first granddaughter, raised to keep promises and make fists.

The thing about teaching mobile students, regardless of setting—homelessness, foster care, migration purgatory—is that part of the pedagogy is the practice of saying goodbye. The absolute worst goodbyes are the ones you never get to say, the kids who disappear overnight or on that one personal day you took to see your mother. I'm lucky. The number of goodbyes I've said to children outweighs the number of goodbyes that disintegrated in my throat. I've hugged and waved and given away my fidgets. I've whispered adiós, ciao, bonne chance, bendición.

My name is Dulce–Marie Flecha, and I am my grandmothers' child.

ROBERTO

Together, Everyone Achieves More

By Roberto Germán

[Verse 1]
We stick together
That's our main focus
Working alone can feel hopeless
Take heed and notice
The dope rhymes we provide to increase your dose
Of an educational lesson that reflects hope
We're reaching, teaching, and preaching by claiming a strong
    thesis
Attracting minds like magnets to make them stick like leeches
We cleanse bad thoughts by using lyrical bleach
And practice rhetorical methods to improve our speech
We're streetwise soldiers who refuse to fold over
Moving like an avalanche
Solid as a boulder
Only way we'll make it in this world is standing firm
And the lesson of the day is that we must learn

[Chorus]
Team Play
Together, Everyone Achieves More
We're breaking down barriers and kicking down doors

Team Play
Set goals that you can achieve
And have faith in your teammates 'cause you got to believe

Team Play
There's no job that we can't handle
The going gets tough but we never dismantle

Team Play
To function within the group
When you're working with the team, you have nothing to lose

When I was eighteen, I understood that education extended beyond the four walls of the traditional classroom. I penned these lyrics while working at Los Amigos after-school program in Lawrence, Massachusetts. One of the things that I loved about my experience at Los Amigos was that it felt like a family, and we had a lot of fun even though it was a job. My supervisor, Tim Donahue, gave me the freedom to introduce my talents and strengths into the curriculum. As a result, it was common practice for me to write songs and poems that I would perform with my cohort of students who were between the ages of nine and twelve years old.

I wrote the song "Together, Everyone Achieves More" for me, Ronald, and Sammy (my friends) to perform. I knew very little about teaching and pedagogy at the time. What I did understand was that they found my approach engaging because it incorporated literary genres that resonated with them, encouraged student voices, and embraced their culture. Additionally, as a

Dominican American from the community, I served as an identifiable role model for the students. They knew I sought to bring the best out of each learner while trying to ensure that the learning environment was full of joy. Even as I write this now, it brings a smile to my face!

THE CULTURE OF WHITE DOMINATION IN SCHOOLS

Before we end this book, let's pause here to talk about some of the most common ways racism shows up in schooling spaces. Actually, let's be real—it shows up everywhere, but since the focus of this book is on school and schooling, we'll stick to that.

Some things can be easily and directly linked to racism. You can see something and hear it and know that it is racism immediately. Other times, many other times, it may not be as obvious. This is because the culture of White domination is so deeply embedded in our society that it's what we think of as normal.

The prevailing culture of our country typically divides people from one another. It exists in our neighborhoods, in the hospitals we go to, the libraries, the public transportation systems, the stores we shop in—it's everywhere, including in our schools. The dominant parts of the culture, things like fear, perfectionism, binary thinking, individualism, and "the worship of the written word," exist in our school systems because they are part of the foundation of our country, and that foundation includes racism and oppression.

In 1999, educator, artist, author, and activist Tema Okun and her colleague Kenneth Jackson Jones published an article titled "White Supremacy Culture." The article laid out information that helps us understand the dominant culture of our institutions and country and how it exists in our everyday lives. (The article has since been updated, and you can read more about it at whitesupremacyculture.info.)

In this book, I use the term **WHITE SUPREMACY** because it is the term we are more familiar with, and I also use the term **WHITE DOMINATION**. My friend Britt Hawthorne taught me that using White domination instead of White supremacy allows us to shift out of the old way of thinking that white people are superior to others. (Britt, like me, is a Black biracial educator and author. They do a lot of work with schools and teachers and help them build more just and equitable, bold and anti-racist spaces.) The term White domination more accurately depicts what is happening in the culture. I also think folks get caught up in the imagery of White supremacists when we talk about White supremacy culture. We know what the Ku Klux Klan and Nazis were like, and we're familiar with the atrocities they inflicted on so many people. White supremacy culture is not the same as White supremacists. White supremacists are individuals and groups who believe that people who are White are supreme and should dominate society. White supremacy culture describes the ways in which colonizers and White folks with power have created Whiteness and the idea that there is a racialized hierarchy with White folks at the top of it. White supremacy and its culture are a construct that defines who is fully human and who is not. In this book we will use the term White domination when we're learning about White supremacy and its culture to help us better understand how dominant this is in our country and society. I hope that gaining a deeper understanding of the culture of White domination will help us use more accurate language, which, I recognize, takes time.

The culture of White domination is inescapable.

Sometimes it's obvious, like when you look around at the people working at your school and notice the majority of the teachers and administrators are White and most of the support staff are Brown and Black folks. Or you might notice that many of the books you are assigned are written by White authors, a lot of whom are men who died years ago. But other times, it might not be so obvious, like when you're feeling rushed to complete an assignment and hand it in on time without understanding the purpose of the work. You might also notice that students who complete their math assignments quickly are rewarded for how fast they worked rather than for the process they used to solve the problem. The culture of White domination is a part of everything, and when we let it be our normal, it divides us from other people and communities. It can even divide us from ourselves. It harms us all, especially BIPOC people and our communities.

Tema Okun reminds us that while "White supremacy culture informs us, it does not define us. It is a construct, and anything constructed can be deconstructed and replaced." Understanding what some of the characteristics are and what they look like in our schools and our communities can help us to resist them and break free of the hold this dominant culture has on us.

What is the purpose of White domination?

The goal of White domination is to divide people from each other. And it makes us afraid of people who are different from us. Racism is a tool of the culture of White domination, just as ableism, transphobia, classism, sexism, antisemitism, Islamophobia, and all the other oppressive -isms and -phobias are.

The culture of White domination is everywhere in everything in society. It's part of the values and belief systems in our daily lives—including our schooling. It has some of us convinced that Whiteness is valuable and in fact has more value than any other race. It targets BIPOC people and communities and harms us all. White domination has shaped what we view as and believe to be normal. Thankfully, what has been constructed can be deconstructed and what we know as normal can change.

White domination has features and attributes, and when you know what they are and how they manifest in our lives, you are better able to resist them.

Let's first define what some* of these characteristics are and what they might look like in school.

Fear is one many people are familiar with. It is an emotion that comes from believing that a person, a group, a place, or

---

* There are other characteristics of White domination culture that I didn't include in this book because they are very similar to the ones we're learning about. Even though they're not here, they do exist in our schools and society.

something else is a threat. Fear comes when you believe that you might experience discomfort or pain, which can cause anxiety and irrational thoughts and actions. Fear is the driving force of White domination. It keeps us on edge, scared, exhausted, angry, and completely disconnected from ourselves and others.

In school, fear shows up in many different ways. It comes in the way history is told through emphasizing conflict and differences among people and countries (often based on different religions, social, and political beliefs). We fear not being the best and being powerless and we fear for our safety. It lives in the ways we're encouraged to compete with one another, whether for the highest grades, for college acceptance, in the sports we play. We are discouraged from naming our fears and don't often learn how to cope with them because there's rarely enough time or space to address our social and emotional well-being in schools.

Perfectionism is believing that someone or something is perfect and without flaws or defects. The idea of being perfect is often based on the rules and culture of the status quo and what is perceived as normal. We can easily fall into the belief that we must strive for perfectionism if we are to be successful and matter in school. Focusing on fixing mistakes and on what needs to be corrected rather than learning from our mistakes can create the false belief that if we are not perfect, we are worthless. And when folks who make few or no mistakes on a project or an assignment are rewarded and praised, we hold the false belief that they are better and more worthy. There is little appreciation and support for recognizing and working through the mistakes together, even when it benefits everyone in the community.

Paternalism is a way of holding power and control over people (individuals, groups, even whole countries) by giving some folks barely enough resources to meet their basic needs and by withholding their rights. It is named after the stereotypical relationship between a father and child. Paternalism limits people's right to autonomy and independence and sets up the belief that the persons/people/organizations who are "helping" are superior and necessary.

We are taught, from the moment we enter schooling spaces, that the adults in charge hold the power. (From the classroom teachers to the school administrators to the school boards, adults hold power when it comes to schooling.) They make all the decisions, set the rules and traditions, and define the standards of success. They determine what we learn, who we learn it with, and when and where we do our learning. Children and students are not often included in the decision-making processes and are encouraged to go along with the status quo even when it does not have their interests and well-being at the center.

The belief that a person can share facts without using personal biases and prejudices, feelings, thoughts, and opinions is *objectivity*. Being objective means a person is without bias or favoritism and is considered neutral.

Schools are sometimes the first places we learn to bottle

up our emotions and try to hold things in. We read textbooks that teach us about horrific histories using plain, unemotional, passive, and neutral language. We are taught to write papers based solely on fact and not to inject any personal opinion or thoughts into them. In our classrooms, we're labeled as *distracted* and *irrational* and *too sensitive* and *destructive* if we express emotions and opinions that are not in alignment with the banality of the typical school day. We're discouraged from expressing outrage when the folks with power reduce our lives to stereotypes, leaving us unsafe in school spaces.

There's a common belief in our country that someone who is more "qualified" than others is a person who is more accomplished, capable, and competent. To be *qualified* means they may have the proper qualifications and requirements that have been defined by the dominant culture of the country (having a college degree, passing certain exams, and so on). However, these qualifications are often not easy to obtain and require the person to have more resources (time, money, energy) and advantages in life.

Binary thinking is a belief that complex ideas and problems can be simplified, that there are only two sides to something, only either/or, right or wrong, good or bad, and so on.

If you've ever taken a true-or-false quiz, you are familiar with either/or thinking. Maybe you've been asked to debate a side of an issue, to choose between using a restroom with a sign that says Male and one that says Female, or told something like "You can either keep talking and miss recess or be quiet and go to recess"—binary thinking is so much a part of the school day. Sometimes in our classrooms we're set up to feel like it's us against them, and there's a divide between students who have different social and personal identities. We're not often encouraged to pause and slow down so we can understand the complexity of what we're being asked to do. Instead, we're asked to simplify things even when they're complicated and deserve our attention and time.

It often feels like people value the *quantity over the quality* of work and relationships. The focus turns to making progress or on the amount of time saved or on the amount of money being made or on the number of words on a paper. When we emphasize the quantity of something over the quality, it means we are choosing to ignore or put aside the quality and standards of what we are doing or creating.

In school, we are often assigned a number of pages to read or a certain number of math equations to solve. The emphasis is often on how much we can get done rather than on what we're actually doing and what we are learning. And once we've completed a reading assignment, we have to write about it with a certain amount of words, even if we need to use fewer or more words to get our point across. In our elementary-school classes, the emphasis on learning to read is about moving up in reading levels rather than on enjoying the process of learning to read and reading new words, sentences, and types of books. The goal is to not miss a day of school and to get good grades and high marks, and those with the most are the ones who are rewarded with accolades, commendations, and praise.

It is often believed that the written word is the most important thing; it can feel like we're actually *worshipping the written word*. Any information, whether it is based in truth or not, is honored and believed if it is written down. Documentation and what is written is valued over what is shared orally and visually. With the emphasis and focus on the written word, the erasure of people and culture occurs.

Often in our classrooms and learning spaces we are taught from textbooks and traditionally published books; nothing else has much value in the lesson, especially if it hasn't been written down. Almost everything, unless we are in a class where we're learning a language that isn't English or in a bilingual classroom, is written in standard American English. Other languages and styles and dialects of English are rarely welcome. And if something isn't grammatically correct, we're made to believe it isn't worth reading. Before we even enter school, our caregivers have to fill out form after form with information about us, and this continues onward. Everything must be written down for it to exist.

Individualism is an emphasis on the importance of being an individual, being independent, and having the ability to be in control of your own self. In our country, the focus is often on the rights and freedoms of individual people rather than on communities as a whole. We place individuals on pedestals and hold the belief that no one else could have done what that one person did.

We're often encouraged to learn and process and work alone in school, and even when we do have group projects, our individual roles are emphasized over the group dynamics. We celebrate individuals who did great things and rarely learn about all the people who supported them and worked alongside them. Whole movements of groups are ignored because we applaud individuals. The emphasis is almost always on what you can accomplish on your own rather than on what you can do to be present and learn in a whole community.

Refusing to believe or accept something or someone and claiming that it is not true is *denial*. Denial shows up in many ways in schools. We're taught histories from a point of view that denies the stories of generations of people. We learn about enslavement without ever reading or hearing stories of those who were enslaved. We learn about World War II and what happened in Europe without learning about how our own country imprisoned Japanese, Japanese Americans, and citizens of Japanese descent in internment camps at the same time. We don't usually learn about racism and genderism and homophobia and all the other oppressive tools used by the culture of White domination, and that very silence is the denial of our lives and our histories. We've heard phrases like "I don't see color!" and "We're all the same!" and "We're all a family!" and while the intent behind these is often to unite people, the impact is that we feel more divided because we're denied our full humanity in spaces.

Upholding the belief that only some have a *right to comfort*, that people in power have the right to emotional, physical, and psychological comfort while others do not, is another characteristic of the culture of White dominance. This sets us up to have little or no tolerance for discomfort or conflict and leads us to avoid those things altogether. The right to comfort often looks like *fear of open conflict,* where being polite, ignoring issues, and reaching compromise are emphasized over working to learn from conflict that arises.

In our classrooms, we're often silenced when we raise issues with anything involving the established traditions and rules. We're told we're being impolite or rude. And then any disruption becomes the fault of the student who raised the issue; no one looks more deeply into why things are the way they are and where inequities exist. When we express any kind of big emotions, like anger, deep sadness, or frustration, we get sent out of class. Teachers and administrators ignore conflict by telling us we can "deal with it later." The emphasis is almost always on what is considered rational (according to the culture of our society). There isn't time or space to restore justice and repair the community when we place the right to comfort for some as more important than accountability to the whole community.

Urgency is a sense of acting quickly that is often emphasized in schools and society. Everything must be tackled with immediacy. Students are often expected to move about the day with urgency. Everything is urgent in school, from the timed math quiz to moving from one class to another. The school day's schedule is packed, with every minute accounted for.

217

We're encouraged to be seated and ready to learn before the bell rings. Reminders to "not waste time" and "keep up the pace" and "finish your work now" are constant in one form or another from elementary school onward. Folks who complete the assignments the fastest are often rewarded and praised.

I'm still working on deconstructing the ways in which White domination exists within me. It's not easy to resist and unlearn the things that seem so "normal" and typical. Spending time learning about my own social and personal identities, where I hold power and where I do not, has helped. Connecting with people who are working on unlearning, undoing, and resisting the culture of White domination has also helped. So has learning more. Reading and listening to other folks who are sharing the ways the culture of White domination has affected their lives and noticing when and where it shows up in me and in the systems I am part of also helps me to deconstruct a little more.

People are dynamic. We are constantly growing and changing, learning and unlearning. We are always becoming who we are.

Throughout this book, my friends and I shared stories about our schooling experiences. We are all folks of the Global Majority. We went to different schools in different parts of the country (and world). We are different ages, genders, races, and ethnicities. We are different religions and speak different home languages. We have all witnessed, experienced, and dealt with

218

racism in schools. Whether it was overt or covert, it's a part of our stories.

The culture of White domination is the underlying constant of so many of our stories because it's a part of the very foundation of our country and the institutions we are a part of.

JOANNA

School Is the World

By Joanna Ho

School was my safe space,
a place that held me to my axis
as the world around me
spun
and spun.

I threw myself into
classes and clubs,
projects and papers,
assignments and activities,
filling my weeks
with passion and purpose.

I trusted school would
teach me to swim in the water,
show me my own power and worth,

fill me with skills and wisdom
to take on the world.

And it did.

But every year I look back and realize school
held up a picture of someone else and told me it was a mirror,
erased me even as it praised me,
filled me full of holes
I'll spend my life working to heal.

School is the world.
And we must take it on.

WHAT COMES NEXT?

What could school look like if our institutions were truly centered on learners of the Global Majority and those who have been historically, systematically, and systemically excluded and marginalized for so long?

Envision what freedom in schools could be.
What does it look like? Sound like? Smell like? Feel like?
What does it mean to be free in any schooling space or situation?
What would you like to learn?
(How do you learn best?)
What do you wish you had learned?
What do you need to unlearn? What do you need to relearn?
It is possible to commit to the daily work of abolishing oppressive systems in our schools? What are some things you can do today? Tomorrow? Next week? Years from now?

How can you take action to reclaim yourself in schooling spaces and situations?

What action can you take to reclaim yourself from the educational system?

Create a vision for the future!

Knowing who you are will help you know what it is you are fighting for. What do you believe in? What do you want for your future? For our future?

How will you bring your whole self into these overwhelmingly unwelcoming spaces when they—by design—fracture us as individuals and divide us as groups?

How can we connect and reconnect with ourselves? Others? The institutions we are part of?

What do our educational institutions need?

And, more importantly, what do we need from these institutions?

How can we work collectively so schools can be places where we actively choose love over fear every single time?

What do we need in order to do this?

How can we get there . . . together?

Schools should be places where we are honored for who we are and not viewed as though we have deficits and are disruptions. Schools should be places where we can connect with one another and dream and work together to abolish oppressive systems. Schools and schooling situations should be spaces and moments when we can be our bravest and boldest selves.

RESOURCES

If you would like to opt out of state standardized testing, you and your caregivers may send a letter to your school's principal.

Sample letter to opt out of standardized testing:

Dear [name of teacher, guidance counselor, principal],

We wanted to let you know that our child [name of student] *will not take part in any* [names of state standardized tests] *testing this year.*

Our decision to opt out is not a reflection of the school or the amazing teachers who work so hard to give our children the best education possible. It is based on the fact that we feel that there is an overemphasis on standardized testing, and that the [names of tests] *work to aggravate educational inequities, which we would prefer not to be a part of this year.*

We appreciate that some educators feel concerned by students opting out and hope effective action will be taken to stop students from being shamed or pressured on this issue directly from adults or indirectly through other students. Thank you for your support on this. Please arrange for [name of student] *to have a productive educational experience during the testing period.*

As per the state's suggestion,* we encourage the test administrator to document this refusal and keep it on record in case questions arise about the school's participation rate.

We are grateful to be part of the school community.

Sincerely,
[names of caregivers here]

---

* Please check with your state's guidance on opting out. This can usually be found with a search using the keywords *how to opt out of* [name of tests].

If you'd like to opt out of having your information collected on the JAMRS (Joint Advertising, Market Research and Studies), you may send a letter to

*Joint Advertising Market Research and Studies (JAMRS)**
Attn: Survey Project Manager
4800 Mark Center Drive, Suite 06J25
Alexandria, VA 22350-4000

To the Direct Program Marketing Officer:

Please remove my name and information from the JAMRS military recruitment database. [You may add anything else you'd like. For example, "The collection and distribution of this information violates my privacy and I do not believe the Department of Defense should do this."]

Below, find the data to be removed:
[full name]
[date of birth]
[full address, including city and state]

[signature including date]

---

* Please search for the JAMRS contact information before you send this, as information can change.

If you are under eighteen years old, your caregivers may need to sign the letter too.

If you'd like to opt of being recruited by the military, your school should provide you with a form that you can complete and sign with your caregivers/guardians. If your school does not have a form, which it should, contact your school district or the local chapter of the ACLU for a form.

RECOMMENDED READS

An Abolitionist's Handbook: 12 Steps to Changing Yourself and the World
by Patrisse Cullors

ACLU Know Your Rights Handbook
by American Civil Liberties Union (ACLU)

All My Rage by Sabaa Tahir

America Redux: Visual Stories from Our Dynamic History
by Ariel Aberg-Riger

The Autobiography of Malcolm X as told to Alex Haley
by Malcolm X

Blue Ink Tears: A Collection of Poems by Roberto Germán

The Brave by James Bird

Call and Response: The Story of Black Lives Matter
    by Veronica Chambers

Charisma's Turn: A Graphic Novel
    by Monique Couvson (formerly Monique W. Morris)

Disability Visibility: First-Person Stories from the Twenty-First Century
    edited by Alice Wong

Emergent Strategy: Shaping Change, Changing Worlds
    by adrienne maree brown

Freedom Is a Constant Struggle: Ferguson, Palestine, and the Foundations
    of a Movement by Angela Y. Davis

Ghosts in the Schoolyard: Racism and School Closings on Chicago's South
    Side by Eve L. Ewing

Hands by Torrey Maldonado

The History of Institutional Racism in U.S. Public Schools
    by Susan DuFresne

How the World Is Passed: A Reckoning with the History of Slavery Across
    America by Clint Smith

Illustrated Black History: Honoring the Iconic and the Unseen
by George McCalman

I'm Still Here: Black Dignity in a World Made for Whiteness
by Austin Channing Brown

I'm Still Here (Adapted for Young Readers): Loving Myself in a World Not Made for Me by Austin Channing Brown

Know Your Rights and Claim Them: A Guide for Youth
by Amnesty International, Angelina Jolie, and Geraldine Van Bueren

Patron Saints of Nothing by Randy Ribay

Punished for Dreaming: How School Reform Harms Black Children and How We Heal by Bettina L. Love

Pushout: The Criminalization of Black Girls in Schools
by Monique Couvson (formerly Monique W. Morris)

Sigh, Gone: A Misfit's Memoir of Great Books, Punk Rock, and the Fight to Fit In by Phuc Tran

The Silence that Binds Us by Joanna Ho

This Book Is Anti-Racist by Tiffany Jewell

The Twenty-One: The True Story of the Youth Who Sued the U.S. Government Over Climate Change by Elizabeth Rusch

Unbelonging by Gayatri Sethi

Unequal: A Story of America
by Michael Eric Dyson and Marc Favreau

We Gon' Be Alright: Notes on Race and Resegregation by Jeff Chang

We Want to Do More Than Survive: Abolitionist Teaching and the Pursuit of Educational Freedom by Bettina L. Love

What the Fact?: Finding the Truth in All the Noise
by Dr. Seema Yasmin

Why Are All the Black Kids Sitting Together in the Cafeteria?: And Other Conversations About Race by Beverly Daniel Tatum, PhD

Women, Race & Class by Angela Y. Davis

ACKNOWLEDGMENTS

Thank you.

Thank you to all the students, educators, librarians, administrators, and community members who read the books I write. While book bans continue to be on the rise and the truth is questioned and feared, I am grateful to all the readers who seek the truth and move through the word with love.

This book has been in the works for many years. During the pandemic, I spoke at a virtual conference for teachers where I talked about my schooling experiences. While I was talking, I said, "Just about everything I learned about racism I learned in school." I had to pause after that—we all did—because . . . wow! It was absolutely true. Thank you to the EdCollab for sparking this conversation I didn't know needed to happen.

Thank you to many of the educators who taught me throughout my schooling journey—but especially Mrs. Campbell, Mrs.

Effler, Mrs. Rosa Clark, Señor Ogden, Ms. Quigley, Ms. Kirkland, Mr. Sturge, Mr. Belanger, Señora Meier, and Professor Jeff Claus.

I am forever in awe of the folks who contributed to this book. Thank you for saying "yes" and sharing your stories with the world—Amelia A. Sherwood, August, Aspen Mae, David Ryan Barcega Castro-Harris, Dulce-Marie Flecha, Emmanuel, Gary Gray Jr., Gayatri Sethi, James Bird, Joanna Ho, Liz Kleinrock, Lorena Germán, Minh Lê, Ozy Aloziem, Patrick Harris II, Randy Ribay, Rebekah Borucki, Roberto Germán, shea wesley martin, and Torrey Maldonado.

Many thanks go to the friends who answered my questions of "Do you remember . . . ?" and "Did this really happen . . . ?" and to the *Syracuse Post-Standard* and *Syracuse Herald-Journal* archives for affirming memories and broadening my historical knowledge of the city where I grew up. Thanks to my mom and my nana for keeping the memories in paper form. Thanks to my twin for the shared experience with a different perspective.

Appreciating the many playlists, albums, and songs that brought me back to specific times and places and accompanied me in the many drafts and revisions of this book (especially the Cranberries, REM, Boyz II Men, TLC, Bright Eyes/Conor Oberst, Mary J. Blige, Black Eyes, Dr. Dog, the Roots, and the Clash).

Thank you to my incredible agent, Ayesha Pande—I'm so grateful to have you on my side! And, thanks to the folks at APL and PLM.

Thank you to the Versify and Clarion Books team, especially Weslie Turner, who reminds me that it's okay to STET and has believed in this book from the start. Also, shout-out to the copyeditor who not only polished this book but dropped grammar knowledge nuggets throughout. Thank you to George McCalman, Aliena Cameron, and Ayana Miyoshi for breathing some beauty and life into this book (and appreciating my goofiness)!

And, finally, a special thanks goes to my family. Thanks to my mom for choosing our neighborhood schools. Thanks to my twin for championing what I do. Thanks to my nana for your memory keeping. (You are missed every day.) Thanks to my husband for holding *all* the things together, the many cups of tea, and all the things. Thanks to my kiddos for their patience, jokes, and snuggles. Thanks to the grandparents, friends, aunties, uncle, and cousins who have helped out when I've been away, glued to my computer, and lost in thought. Thank you. I love you.

REFERENCES

WHAT I LEARNED ABOUT MY LABEL

- Pew Research Center. "Chapter 1: Race and Multiracial Americans in the U.S. Census." 11 June 2015. https://www.pewresearch.org/social -trends/2015/06/11/chapter-1-race-and-multiracial-americans -in-the-u-s-census/.
- Riede, Paul. "Integration Plan Outgrowing Limits." *The Post-Standard*, 3 February 1992, A6.
- McGuire, Dan. "Integration Is Off Balance In 3 City Schools." *Syracuse Herald-Journal*, 3 November 1998, E3.
- Nolan, Maureen. "District Labels Irk Students. Tags That Were Issued for Student Planners Draw Criticism at Corcoran. The Superintendent Agrees That Racial Identification Served No Useful Purpose." *The Post-Standard*, 9 October 1997, Local News Section.
- Jewell, Tiara. "I'm A Multiracial American." *Syracuse Herald-Journal*, 5 March 1998, HJ Section.

WHAT I LEARNED ABOUT WHITENESS

- American Council on Education. "Participation in Advanced Placement." https://www.equityinhighered.org/indicators/secondary

-school-completion/participation-in-advanced-placement/.

- The Education Trust. "Black and Latino Students Shut Out of Advanced Coursework Opportunities." 9 January 2020. https://edtrust.org/press-release/black-and-latino-students-shut-out-of-advanced-coursework-opportunities/.
- Pottiger, Maya. "Black Students Made Up Smallest Percentage of Enrollment in Advanced Placement Classes." *Word In Black*, 23 September 2021. https://wordinblack.com/2021/09/black-students-made-up-smallest-percentage-of-enrollment-in-advanced-placement-classes/.
- Institute of Education Sciences/National Center for Education Statistics. "Retention, Suspension, and Expulsion." February 2019. https://nces.ed.gov/programs/raceindicators/indicator_rda.aspn.
- USA Facts. "Black students are more likely to be punished than white students." 17 September 2021. https://usafacts.org/articles/black-students-more-likely-to-be-punished-than-white-students/.
- ProPublica. "Syracuse City School District." October 2018. https://projects.propublica.org/miseducation/district/3628590.
- National Information Center for Higher Education Policymaking and Analysis. "College-Going Rates of High School Graduates—Directly from High School." http://www.higheredinfo.org/dbrowser/?year=2018&level=nation&mode=data&state=&submeasure=63.
- Doran, Elizabeth. "See Onondaga Country 2021–2022 high school graduation rates." Syracuse.com, 6 February 2023. https://www.syracuse.com/schools/2023/02/see-onondaga-county-2021-2022-high-school-graduation-rates-chart.html.
- Institute of Education Sciences/National Center for Education Statistics. "Fast Facts: High School Graduation Rates." https://nces.ed.gov/fastfacts/display.asp?id=805.
- Ried, Paul. "Report: Only 37 percent of New York high school freshmen become college- and career-ready within four years." Syracuse.com, 15 June 2011. https://www.syracuse.com/news/2011/06/are_high_school_grads_college-.html.
- Institute of Education Sciences/National Center for Education Statistics. "Fast Facts: Immediate Transition to College." https://nces.ed.gov/fastfacts/display.asp?id=51.

WHAT RACISM IS

- Crossroads: Antiracism Organizing and Training. https://crossroadsantiracism.org.

- Federal Bureau of Prisons. "Inmate Race." 1 April 2023. https://www .bop.gov/about/statistics/statistics_inmate_race.jsp.
- Gramlich, John. "The gap between the number of blacks and whites in prison is shrinking." Pew Research Center, 30 April 2019. https:// www.pewresearch.org/fact-tank/2019/04/30/shrinking-gap -between-number-of-blacks-and-whites-in-prison/.
- Prison Policy Initiative. "Race and Ethnicity." https://www.prisonpolicy .org/research/race_and_ethnicity/.
- Kaiser Family Foundation. kff.org/racial-equity-and-health-policy/.
- "Health Effects of Gentrification." Centers for Disease Control and Prevention. https://www.cdc.gov/healthyplaces/healthtopics /gentrification.htm.
- "'Mayo, Aleeya. Distinctively Black names' still get fewer callbacks for job applications." *Business Insider*, 30 July 2021. https://www .businessinsider.com/racial-discrimination-the-job-market -study-black-names-applications-2021-7.
- Porter, Eduardo. "Who Discriminates in Hiring? A New Study Can Tell." *New York Times*, 29 July 2021. https://www.nytimes.com /2021/07/29/business/economy/hiring-racial-discrimination.html.
- While a few Pacific Islander Asian American women made close to or a little more than White men, most do not. Japanese women made ninety-five cents, Filipino women made eighty-three cents, Fijian women made sixty-six cents, Hmong women made sixty cents, and Burmese women made fifty-two cents. (https://www.americanprogress .org/article/women-of-color-and-the-wage-gap/.)
- Bleiweis, Robin, Jocelyn Frye, and Rose Khattar. "Women of Color and the Wage Gap." The Center for American Progress, 17 November 2021. https://www.americanprogress.org/article/women-of-color -and-the-wage-gap/.
- Moslimani, Mohamad, Christine Tamie, Abby Budiman, Luis Noe-Bustamante, and Lauren Mora. "Facts About the U.S. Black Popu-lation." Pew Research Group, 2 March 2023. https://www.pewresearch .org/social-trends/fact-sheet/facts-about-the-us-black-population/.
- "Popular and Pervasive Stereotypes of African Americans." National Museum of African American History and Culture. https://nmaahc .si.edu/explore/stories/popular-and-pervasive-stereotypes -african-americans.
- https://www.washingtonpost.com/news/wonk/wp/2017/12/13/ news-media-offers-consistently-warped-portrayals-of-black -families-study-finds/.

- "California Department of Education Releases New Attendance Data to Help School Districts Address Chronic Absenteeism." California Department of Education, 10 November 2020. https://www.cde.ca.gov/nr/ne/yr20/yr20rel92.asp.
- "The Racial Gap in Attendance in Public Schools." The Journal of Blacks in Higher Education, 4 January 2021. https://jbhe.com/2021/01/the-racial-gap-in-attendance-and-absenteeism-in-public-schools/.

MY HOME CITY

- When I started my schooling journey (in the 1980s), the population of my home city was just over 170,000. Currently, it is a little over 145,000 people. (https://population.us/ny/syracuse/.)
- https://goldensnowball.com.
- https://en.wikipedia.org/wiki/Golden_Snowball_Award.
- Tampone, Kevin. "Syracuse leads the U.S. with worst child poverty among bigger cities, census says." Syracuse.com, 17 March 2022. https://www.syracuse.com/data/2022/03/syracuse-leads-the-us-with-worst-child-poverty-among-bigger-cities-census-says.html.
- https://cnyvitals.org/poverty/.

MY CHILDHOOD NEIGHBORHOOD

- Tampone, Kevin. "Syracuse leads the U.S. with worst child poverty among bigger cities, census says." Syracuse.com, 17 March 2022. https://www.syracuse.com/data/2022/03/syracuse-leads-the-us-with-worst-child-poverty-among-bigger-cities-census-says.html.
- https://www.syracuse.com/data/2022/10/poverty-in-syracuse-new-numbers-show-citys-grim-ranking-in-family-income-in-us.html.
- Tampone, Kevin. "Poverty in Syracuse: New numbers show city's grim ranking in family income in U.S." Syracuse.com, 3 October 2022. https://www.syracuse.com/data/2022/09/child-poverty-improves-in-syracuse-its-still-among-highest-in-us-census-says.html.
- Benson, Craig. "Poverty Rate of Children Higher Than National Rate, Lower for Older Populations." 4 October 2022. https://www.census.gov/library/stories/2022/10/poverty-rate-varies-by-age-groups.html.

- Burns, Kalee, Liana Fox, and Danielle Wilson. "Expansions to Child Tax Credit Contributed to 46% Decline in Child Poverty Since 2020." 13 September 2022. https://www.census.gov/library/stories/2022/09/record-drop-in-child-poverty.html.
- National Center for Education Statistics (2023). "Characteristics of Children's Families. Condition of Education." U.S. Department of Education, Institute of Education Sciences. https://nces.ed.gov/programs/coe/indicator/cce.
- National Poverty in America Awareness Month: January 2023, https://www.census.gov/newsroom/stories/poverty-awareness-month.html.
- WIC, which stands for Women, Infants & Children, is a federal government program that provides support, assistance, and access to healthy foods and programs around nutrition for women and young children. (https://www.signupwic.com.)

WHAT I LEARNED ABOUT MAGNET SCHOOLS

- Schaeffer, Katherine. "America's public school teachers are far less racially and ethnically diverse than their students." 10 December 2021. https://www.pewresearch.org/fact-tank/2021/12/10/americas-public-school-teachers-are-far-less-racially-and-ethnically-diverse-than-their-students/.
- "Race and Ethnicity of Public School Teachers and Their Students." September 2020. https://nces.ed.gov/pubs2020/2020103/index.asp.
- National Teacher and Principal Survey. "Percentage distribution of public school principals, by race/ethnicity and state: 2017–18." https://nces.ed.gov/surveys/ntps/tables/ntps1718_19110501_a1s.asp.
- Waldrip, Donald. "A Brief History of Magnet Schools." https://magnet.edu/brief-history-of-magnets.
- Herron, Frank. "The Pull of Magnet Schools." *Syracuse Herald-Journal*, 22 January 1992, A1.
- Rice, Dale. "Board Adopts Mandatory Busing." *The Post-Standard*, 28 May 1976.
- Chen, Grace. "What Is A Magnet School?" *Public School Review*, 5 August 2019. https://www.publicschoolreview.com/blog/what-is-a-magnet-school.
- Hind, Harold. "Drawn to Success: How Do Integrated Magnet Schools

Work?" *Reimagining Integration Diverse and Equitable Schools*, February 2017. https://rides.gse.harvard.edu/files/gse-rides/files/rides_-_drawn_to _success_how_do_integrated_magnet_schools_work.pdf.

- Rice, Dale. "Nyquist 'Politically Astute.'" *The Post-Standard*, 30 May 1977.
- Rice, Dale. "Voluntary Setup Faces Trial Run." *The Post-Standard*, 17 May 1976.
- McGuire, Dan. "Integration is Off Balance in 3 City Schools." *Syracuse Herald-Journal*, 3 November 1988, E3.
- The New York Civil Liberties Union. "The I-81 Story." 12 March 2021. https://www.nyclu.org/en/campaigns/i-81-story.
- Congress for the New Urbanism. "Syracuse: I-81." https://www.cnu .org/highways-boulevards/campaign-cities/syracuse.
- Carillo, Sequoia, and Pooja Salhorta. "The U.S. student population is more diverse, but schools are still highly segregated." NPR, 14 July 2022. https://www.npr.org/2022/07/14/1111060299/school-segregation -report.
- Riede, Paul. "Integration Plan Outgrowing Limits." *The Post-Standard*, 3 February 1992, A6.
- Martin, Courtney. *Learning In Public: Lessons for Racially Divided America from My Daughter's School*. New York: Little Brown, 2021.
- Ansell, Susan E. "Achievement Gap." *Education Week*, 7 July 2011. https://www.edweek.org/leadership/achievement-gap/2004/09.
- Scyster, Rhianna. "Achievement Gap vs. Opportunity Gap." LinkedIn, 1 December 2022. https://www.linkedin.com/pulse/achievement -gap-vs-opportunity-rhianna-scyster?trk=public_profile _article_view.
- Ladson-Billings, Gloria. "From the Achievement Gap to the Education Debt: Understanding Achievement in U.S. Schools." *Educational Researcher* 35, no. 7 (October, 2006), 3-12. https://www.jstor.org/sta ble/3876731.
- Yates, Mike. "Opinion: Let's Stop Calling It an 'Achievement Gap' When It's Really an Opportunity Gap." 17 July 2018. https://www .weareteachers.com/stop-calling-it-an-achievement-gap/.

WHAT I LEARNED ABOUT ELEMENTARY SCHOOL

- Neils, Karen. "2 Syracuse Schools Cited As Deficient." *The Post-Standard*, 19 December 1989, A1.

- District administration claimed the school to be "deficient" because the reading and math test scores were lower than in other schools.
- My home city sits on the unceded land that is the homeland of the Onondagas, who are a part of the Haudenosaunee Nation.
- DARE is a program that offers skills to kids from pre-K-12 that help them to avoid drug use and abuse, violence, and gang involvement. The program is led by police officers who give lessons to kids in schools. The program has been in existence since 1983. https://dare.org.
- Onondaga Environmental Institute. "History." Accessed 8 April 2023. https://www.oei2.org/our-watershed/history/.
- Onondaga Nation. "Onondaga Lake." Accessed 8 April 2023. https://www.onondaganation.org/land-rights/onondaga-lake/.

MY MIDDLE SCHOOL

- Rice, Dale. "South Side Parents Suing Board." *The Post-Standard*, 6 January 1977.
- Rice, Dale. "Open Enrollment Doesn't Work." *The Post-Standard*, 2 May 1977.
- Saiz, Laurel. "Quadrant Quandary Still Unresolved." *The Post-Standard*, 21 May 1977.
- Riede, Paul. "Integration Plan Outgrowing Limits." *The Post-Standard*, 3 February 1992.
- Reide, Paul. "City Schools Hope to Alter Program for Integration." *The Post-Standard*, 5 December 1992.

WHAT I LEARNED ABOUT TRACKING

- Kohli, Sonali and Quartz. "Modern-Day Segregation in Public Schools." *The Atlantic*, 18 November 2014. https://www.theatlantic.com/education/archive/2014/11/modern-day-segregation-in-public-schools/382846/.
- Gallardo, Elia V. "Hierarchy and Discrimination: Tracking in Public Schools." *Chicana/o Latina/o Law Review*, 1994. https://escholarship.org/uc/item/1vj0h4ww.
- Barrington, Kate. "The Pros and Cons of Tracking in Schools." *Public School Review*, 9 December 2020. https://www.publicschoolreview.com/blog/the-pros-and-cons-of-tracking-in-schools.

- Wexler, Natalie. "To End High School Tracking, We Need to End Tracking In Elementary School." *Forbes*, 10 August 2019. https://www.forbes .com/sites/nataliewexler/2019/08/10/to-end-high-school-trackingwe -need-to-end-tracking-in-elementary-school/?sh=47361bea49a8.
- U.S. Department of Education. "Student Assignment in Elementary and Secondary Schools & Title VI." September 1998. https://www2 .ed.gov/about/offices/list/ocr/docs/tviassgn.html.

MY HIGH SCHOOL

- Onondaga Historical Association. "December 1965: Corcoran High School Dedication." https://www.cnyhistory.org/2015/12/corcoran/.

WHAT I LEARNED DURING MY SOPHOMORE YEAR

- Jonathan Larson (b. February 4, 1960 d. January 25, 1996) was a playwright and composer and is most known for his musicals *RENT* and *Tick, Tick ... Boom! RENT* is a rock musical that debuted off-Broadway in 1996 (on the same day as Larson's death.) The musical is about a group of friends living in New York City at the end of the millennium who are struggling with being able to pay rent, with love, and with life.

WHAT I LEARNED ABOUT SUICIDE

- Johnson, Steven Ross. "Study: Adolescents Accounted for Larger Share of Suicides in 2020." *U.S. News & World Report*, 25 April 2022. https://www.usnews.com/news/health-news/articles/2022-04-25 /study-shows-higher-share-of-adolescent-suicides-in-2020.
- "AAP-AACAP-CHA Declaration of a National Emergency in Child and Adolescent Mental Health." American Academy of Pediatrics, 19 October 2021. https://www.aap.org/en/advocacy/child-and -adolescent-healthy-mental-development/aap-aacap-cha -declaration-of-a-national-emergency-in-child-and-adolescent -mental-health/.
- The Trevor Project. "National Survey on LGBTQ Youth Mental

Health 2019." Accessed 8 April 2023. https://www.thetrevorproject
.org/survey-2019/section=Introduction.

- Abrams, Zara. "Sounding the alarm on black youth suicide." American
  Psychological Association, 28 January 2020. https://www.apa.org/news
  /apa/2020/black-youth-suicide.
- "Disparities in Suicide." Centers for Disease Control and Prevention,
  9 May 2023. https://www.cdc.gov/suicide/facts/disparities-in-suicide
  .html#print.
- "After a student suicide." Centre for Suicide Prevention, 10 April 2019.
  https://www.suicideinfo.ca/local_resource/after-a-student-suicide
  /#commsplan.
- Esposito, Lisa. "How Schools Cope After a Tragedy Like Suicide."
  U.S. News & World Report, 24 December 2014. https://health.usnews
  .com/health-news/health-wellness/articles/2014/12/24/how-schools
  -cope-after-a-tragedy-like-suicide.

WHAT I LEARNED ABOUT MILITARY RECRUITMENT

- Syracuse University Project Advance: https://supa.syr.edu.
- UNESCO. "Cuba." https://uis.unescoorg/en/country/cu.
- The World Bank. "Literacy rate, adult total (% of people ages 15 and
  above)." https://data.worldbank.org/indicator/SE.ADT.LITR.ZS.
- Syracuse City School District. "New York State Graduation Requirements." https://www.syracusecityschools.com/districtpage
  .cfm?pageid=524#:~:text=22-,Regents%20Diploma,of%20the%20
  CDOS%20Commencement%20Credential.
- Colleges and universities use the FAFSA application to determine
  what type of financial aid students are eligible for (and how much they
  might receive). Anyone who needs federal grants, student loans, or
  work study needs to complete the Free Application For Student Aid
  and can do so via the website: studentaid.gov.
- Burrelli, David F. and Jody Feder. "Military Recruitment On High
  School and College Campuses: A Policy and Legal Analysis."
  Congressional Research Service, 22 September 2009, 1-12.
- Wikipedia. "United States Army Recruiting Command." Accessed
  8 April 2023. https://en.wikipedia.org/wiki/United_States_Army_
  Recruiting_Command.
- Corcione, Adryan. "The Military Targets Youth for Recruitment,

244

Especially at Poor Schools." *Teen Vogue*, 22 January 2019. https://www
.teenvogue.com/story/the-military-targets-youth-for-recruitment.
- Department of Defense, Office of the Deputy Assistant Secretary of
Defense for Military Community and Family Policy, under contract
with ICF. "2017 Demographics: Profile of the Military Community."
https://download.militaryonesource.mil/12038/MOS/Reports
/2017-demographics-report.pdf.
- Selective Service System. "History of the Selective Service System."
https://www.sss.gov/history-and-records/.
- Selective Service System. "Who Needs to Register." https://www.sss
.gov/register/who-needs-to-register/.
- Title I is a federal program that provides some funding to schools
that have a high percentage of students who are living in poverty or
low-income homes. A little less than half of the public schools in the
country receive Title I funding from the government.
- U.S. Department of Defense. "Department of Defense Releases the
President's Fiscal Year 2024 Budget." 13 March 2023. https://www
.defense.gov/News/Releases/Release/Article/3326875/department
-of-defense-releases-the-presidents-fiscal-year-2024-defense
-budget/#:~:text=On%20March%209%2C%202023%2C%20the,
billion%20more%20than%20FY%202022.
- JAMRS: Department of Defense. "Recruiting Database." https://
jamrs.defense.gov/Recruiting-Database/.
- JAMRS: Department of Defense. "Welcome to Joint Advertising,
Market Research & Studies." https://jamrs.defense.gov/.
- New York Civil Liberties Union: ACLU of New York. "Protect Your Rights:
Opt Out!" https://www.nyclu.org/en/protect-your-rights-opt-out.
- American Civil Liberties Union. "Affiliates: Find Your ACLU."
https://www.aclu.org/about/affiliates.

WHAT I LEARNED DURING MY SENIOR YEAR

- Wikipedia. "'Save the Best for Last.'" Accessed 8 April 2023.
https://en.wikipedia.org/wiki/Save_the_Best_for_Last.
- Wikipedia. "'1999' (Prince song)." Accessed 8 April 2023.
https://en.wikipedia.org/wiki/1999_(Prince_song).
- Wikipedia. "Blazing Saddles." Accessed 8 April 2023. https://en
.wikipedia.org/wiki/Blazing_Saddles.

WHAT I LEARNED ABOUT WEAPONS SEARCHES

- Nolan, Maureen and Paul Riede. "Cappa Ok'd Arms Search." *Syracuse Herald American*, 8 November 1998, A1.
- Nolan, Maureen. "School Search Angers Teens: Some say district should not have searched all Corcoran High School students for weapons." *The Post-Standard*, 6 November 1998, A1.
- "Cappa: Past fights led to search the superintendent told parents safety became a concern after hearing that weapons might be brought to Corcoran High." *The Post-Standard*, 19 November 1998, Neighbors, Syracuse Section, 12.
- Cornell Law School. "Amdt.4.5.5.6 School Searches." https://www .law.cornell.edu/constitution-conan/amendment-4/school-searches.
- United States Supreme Court. *Facts and Case Summary for New Jersey v. T.L.O.*, 393, 15 January 1985, 325–469. Library of Congress. https://tile. loc.gov/storage-services/service/ll/usrep/usrep469 /usrep469325/usrep469325.pdf.
- ACLU of Southern California. "Searches of Students." Accessed 8 April 2023. https://www.myschoolmyrights.com/rights/searches -of-students/.
- Mass.gov. "Juvenile Justice–Constitutional Considerations." Accessed 8 April 2023. https://www.mass.gov/service-details/juvenile-justice -constitutional-considerations#:~:text=%22reasonable%20suspicion %22%20is%20%22a,do%20not%20provide%20reasonable%20 suspicion.
- Ehlenberger, Kate R. "The Rights to Search Students." Association for Supervision and Curriculum Development (ASCD), 1 December 2001. https://www.acsd.org/el/articles/the-right-to-search-students.
- National Youth Rights Association. "Student Rights: Your rights don't stop at the schoolhouse gate." Accessed 8 April 2023. https:// www.youthrights.org/issues/student-rights/.

WHAT I LEARNED ABOUT STUDENTS' RIGHTS

- United States Supreme Court. *Tinker v. Des Moines School District* 469 (24 February 1969): 503–526. Library of Congress. https:// tile.loc.gov/storage-services/service/ll/usrep/usrep393/usrep393503/ usrep393503.pdf.

- American Civil Liberties Union. "Tinker v. Des Moines–Landmark Supreme Court Ruling On Behalf of Student Expression." Accessed 8 April 2023. https://www.aclu.org/other/tinker-v-des-moines-landmark-supreme-court-ruling-behalf-student-expression.
- American Civil Liberties Union. "Know Your Rights Students' Rights." Accessed 8 April 2023. https://www.aclu.org/know-your-rights/students-rights.
- School House Connection. "McKinney-Vento Act: Quick Reference." https://schoolhouseconnection.org/mckinney-vento-act/.

WHAT I LEARNED DURING MY FIRST YEAR OF COLLEGE

- Wells College. "Mission and Honor Code." https://www.wells.edu/about/mission-honor-code.
- Wells College. "Wells College Ghost Stories." Accessed 9 January 2023. https://www.wells.edu/library/find-resources/wells-college-archives/wells-college-ghost-stories.
- Wells College Community Handbook. "Wells College Traditions." https://global.wells.edu/ICS/icsfs/4519-Watermarked_pages.pdf?target=1240fa7d-81c8-4eb7-857e-5533848a3047.
- Wells College. "Traditions." https://www.wells.edu/student-life/traditions.

WHAT I LEARNED ABOUT *MALCOLM X* AND *THELMA & LOUISE*

- Barron, Kaelyn. "The Literary Canon: What's In It, and Who Makes the List?" TCK Publishing. https://www.tckpublishing.com/the-literary-canon/.
- Morris, Wesley. "Who Gets to Decide What Belongs in the 'Canon'?" *New York Times*, 30 May 2018. https://www.nytimes.com/2018/05/30/magazine/who-gets-to-decide-what-belongs-in-the-canon.html.
- Gibson, Caitlyn. "25 Years Ago, *Thelma & Louise* was a radical statement. Sadly, it still is." *The Washington Post*, 20 April 2016. https://www.washingtonpost.com/lifestyle/style/25-years-ago-thelma-and-louise-was-a-radical-statement-sadly-it-still-is/2016/04/20/9abf1ea6-0256-11e6-9203-7b8670959b88_story.html.

- Gorr, Sarah. "*Thelma and Louise*: Opening Statement." *The Cinessential*, 15 August 2016. http://www.thecinessential.com /thelma-and-louise-opening-statement.
- Wikipedia. "1991 in Film." Accessed 8 April 2023. https://en .wikipedia.org/wiki/1991_in_film.
- Wikipedia. "*Malcolm X* (1992 film)." Accessed 8 April 2023. https:// en.wikipedia.org/wiki/Malcolm_X_(1992_film).
- Sterritt, David. "Behind the *Malcolm X* Film: A Need to Set Things Straight." *The Christian Science Monitor*, 24 November 1992. https:// www.csmonitor.com/1992/1124/24011.html.
- Wikipedia. "Alex Haley." Accessed 8 April 2023. https://en.wikipedia .org/wiki/Alex_Haley.

WHAT I LEARNED DURING MY LAST YEAR OF COLLEGE

- U.S. Census Bureau. "Real Median Household Income by Race and Hispanic Origin: 1967 to 2020." https://www.census.gov/content /dam/Census/library/visualizations/2021/demo/p60-273/figure2.pdf.
- National Council on Aging. "The American Indian/Alaska Natives: Key Demographics and Characteristics." 10 January 2023. https:// www.ncoa.org/article/american-indians-and-alaska-natives-key -demographics-and-characteristics.

ABOUT THE CONTRIBUTORS

(in order of appearance)

AMELIA A. SHERWOOD is a Black mama and anti-racist educator living on Quinnipiac land, but you may know it as New Haven, Connecticut. She is the founder of Sankofa Learning Center, an African-centered Montessori program.

RANDY RIBAY was born in the Philippines and raised in the Midwest. He is the award-winning author of the YA novels *An Infinite Number of Parallel Universes*, *After the Shot Drops*, and *Patron Saints of Nothing*, which was selected as a National Book Award finalist. He earned his BA in English literature from the University of Colorado at Boulder and his master's degree in language and literacy from Harvard Graduate School of Education. He currently lives in the San Francisco Bay Area with his wife, child, and catlike dog.

REBEKAH BORUCKI is a mixed-race autistic mother-to-five, grandmother-to-one, self-help and children's author, and the founder and president of Row House Publishing. She is driven by a commitment to make wellness, self-learning, and literacy tools available to all and to help others recover the freedoms stolen from them by white supremacy through activism that centers Black liberation and trans rights. She lives with her family in her native state, New Jersey.

ROBERTO GERMÁN is a Dominican American author, poet, and spoken word artist. He was born in Lawrence, Massachusetts, to immigrant parents. As the Executive Director of Multicultural Classroom, he supports schools and organizations with strategies for anti-bias and anti-racist teaching and learning. He is driven by integrity, faith, family, justice, and more. His work is reflective of these values, characterized by passion, supporting young people, and a dedication to excellence. His writing has been featured in *Raising Antiracist Children: A Practical Parenting Guide,*

Speaking for Ourselves, Edutopia, and others. His first poetry book, *Blue Ink Tears*, focuses on identity, love, relationships, and more. Currently, he lives in Tampa, Florida, with his wife and three children.

MINH LÊ is the award-winning author of picture books, including *The Blur*, *Real to Me*, *Lift* (an Eisner Award nominee), and *Drawn Together* (winner of the 2019 Asian/Pacific American Award for Literature), as well as graphic novels including *Green Lantern: Legacy* and *Enlighten Me*. In addition to writing books, he serves on the board of We Need Diverse Books, is on the faculty of the Hamline University MFA in Writing for Children and Young Adults, and has been a contributor to a variety of publications, including *The Horn Book*, NPR, *HuffPost*, and the *New York Times*. Outside of spending time with his wonderful wife and children at their home in San Diego, his favorite place to be is in the middle of a good book.

EMMANUEL lives in Portland, Oregon. He likes video games, hanging out with his friends, and bears. His favorite season is summer because he loves being in the water.

JAMES BIRD is a First Nations (Ojibwe) author and also an award-winning filmmaker. His films include *Eat Spirit Eat*, *From Above*, *Honeyglue*, *We Are Boats*, and *Wifelike*. When he's not writing, he is rescuing animals with his wife (author Adriana Mather) and their son, Wolf. He is Native American, from the Grand Portage Ojibwe tribe.

LORENA GERMÁN is a two-time nationally awarded Dominican American educator focused on anti-racist and anti-bias education. She's been featured in the *New York Times*, NPR, PBS, *Rethinking Schools*, *EdWeek*, *Learning for Justice* magazine, and more. She published *The Anti Racist Teacher: Reading Instruction Workbook* and *Textured Teaching: A Framework for Culturally Sustaining Practices* about curriculum and lesson development focused on social justice. She's a cofounder of #DisruptTexts and Multicultural Classroom. She is also the Chair of NCTE's Committee Against Racism and Bias in the Teaching of English. She lives in Tampa, Florida, where she is a mami and wife—two of her most important roles.

LIZ KLEINROCK is a Korean American transracial adoptee, queer, Jewish, anti-bias anti-racist educator, facilitator, and author. In 2018, she received the Teaching Tolerance Award for Excellence in Teaching, and in 2019, she delivered her TED Talk, "How to Teach Kids to Talk about Taboo Topics." In the spring of 2021, she released her first book, *Start Here, Start Now: A Guide to Antibias and Antiracist Work in Your School Community*, and is excited to announce the publication of four upcoming children's books. She currently resides in Washington, DC, with her partner and two bunnies.

GARY R. GRAY JR. is an international educator and author from the largest Black community in Canada: Preston, Nova Scotia. He has been teaching internationally for over ten years and is currently a third-grade educator at United Nations School, Hanoi, Vietnam. His picture book, *I'm From*, illustrated by Oge Mora, debuted in 2023. He has an MEd in early elementary pedagogy with a focus on culturally responsive teaching. When he is not in the classroom or storytelling, he is hanging out with family, doodling, searching the latest kicks online, or traveling with his wife, who is also an educator.

AUGUST likes to play basketball, watch basketball, and hang out with friends at basketball games. He lives in Portland, Oregon, home of the Portland Blazers.

PATRICK HARRIS II is a Black queer writer, storyteller, and middle-school humanities teacher. He has won multiple national teaching awards for his leadership and innovation in the classroom, including recognitions from NCTE, ASCD, and ILA. Teaching and creating is only a small part of who he is. He is a big brother, a cat dad, and lover of all things horror. Find Patrick on social media @PresidentPat.

SHEA WESLEY MARTIN is a Black, queer, gender-expansive scholar-teacher raised at the intersection of gospel and go-go. A product of public schooling and community college, they are currently completing their doctoral studies in teaching and learning at The Ohio State University. shea's work explores the ways queer and trans folks of color disrupt and reimagine notions of literacy, archive, and schooling. A former classroom teacher, shea's orientation to their work will be forever informed by some of the dopest youth in Texas, Florida, and Massachusetts.

DAVID RYAN BARCEGA CASTRO-HARRIS exists in this time and space as a result of the love, resilience, and hope of his West African and Filipino ancestors in the face of colonization, enslavement, and impe-rialism. His work as a partner, parent, and family and community member is to build a more just, compas-sionate, and equitable world for future generations. His work as founder of Amplify RJ is to teach the philosophy, practices, and values of Restorative Justice through a lens of abolition, antiracism, and decolonization. He uses digital/social media, facilitated community gatherings, and learning opportunities to help folx understand this work as a relationship-centered way of being, not merely an alternative to punitive approaches to conflict resolution addressing harm.

TORREY MALDONADO was born and raised in Brooklyn's Red Hook housing projects. He has taught in New York City public schools for over twenty-five years, and his fast-paced, compelling stories are inspired by his and his students' expe-riences. His popular young readers novels include *What Lane?*, which garnered many starred reviews and was cited by Oprah Daily and the *New York Times* for being essential to discuss racism and allyship; *Tight*, which won the Christopher Award, was an ALA Notable Book, and was an NPR and *Washington Post* Best

Book of the Year; and his first novel, *Secret Saturdays*, which is an ALA Quick Pick and has stayed in print for over ten years. Learn more at torreymaldonado.com or connect on social media @torreymaldonado.

OZY (OZIOMA) ALOZIEM is an Igbo social work professor and scholar deeply committed to collective liberation, transformational education, racial justice, radical imagination, and healing. She is an award-winning visionary, a well-regarded facilitator and speaker, and has served as a research consultant for numerous organizations across the nation and globe. She spends her time reading, laughing, learning, and loving. You can find her wearing yellow somewhere in the world with her cat, Mushu.

GAYATRI SETHI, PhD, is an educator, writer, and independent consultant. She teaches and writes about social justice, global studies, and comparative education. Born in Tanzania and raised in Botswana, she is of Punjabi descent, multilingual, and polycultural. She reflects on these lifelong experiences of identity, immigration, and belonging in her debut nonfiction book, *Unbelonging*. She is also the cofounder of the Desi KidLit community, an initiative to build solidarity among South Asian diaspora writers for young people. When she is not reading or recommending reads on social media as @desibookaunty, she is envisioning traveling and gathering in community safely again.

DULCE-MARIE FLECHA is an educator and writer from the Bronx, New York, who grew up watching her abuela, Doña Dulce, write poems in ninety-nine-cent-store notebooks. She lives in the Bronx with two cats and many notebooks of her own.

JOANNA HO is the *New York Times* best-selling and award-winning author of many books for kids. She has received the Asian/Pacific American Librarians Association Award for Youth Literature Honor, a Golden Kite Award, an Ezra Jack Keats Honor, and a Golden Poppy Award. She is a writer and educator with a passion for anti-bias, anti-racism, and equity work. She has been an English teacher, a dean, the designer of an alternative-to-prison program, a creator of educator professional development, and a high school vice principal. She lives in the Bay Area, where she survives on homemade chocolate chip cookies, outdoor adventures, and dance parties with her kids. Keep your eyes open for more books to come!

ABOUT THE AUTHOR

TIFFANY JEWELL is a Black biracial writer, twin sister, first-generation American, cisgender mama, and anti-bias antiracist educator. She is the author of the #1 *New York Times* and #1 Indie bestseller *This Book Is Anti-Racist.* Tiffany lives on the homeland of the Pocumtuc, Nipmuck, and Nonotuck with her two young storytellers, her husband, a turtle she's had since she was nine years old, and a small dog with a big personality.